Leckie×Leckie
Scotland's leading educational publishers

Practice Papers for SQA Exams

Higher

Geography

Introduction	3
Topic Index	7
Exam 1	15
Exam 2	35
Exam 3	57
Worked Answers	81

Text © 2010 Bill Dick & Sheena Williamson
Design and layout © 2010 Leckie & Leckie

01/150710

All rights reserved. No part of this publication may be reproduced, stored in a retrieval system, or transmitted in any form or by any means, electronic, mechanical, photocopying, recording or otherwise, without prior permission in writing from Leckie & Leckie Ltd. Legal action will be taken by Leckie & Leckie Ltd against any infringement of our copyright.

The right of Bill Dick & Sheena Williamson to be identified as the Authors of this Work has been asserted by them in accordance with sections 77 and 78 of the Copyright, Designs and Patents Act 1988.

ISBN 978-1-84372-782-8

Published by
Leckie & Leckie
an imprint of HarperCollins*Publishers*
Westerhill Road, Bishopbriggs, Glasgow, G64 2QT
T: 0844 576 8126   F: 0844 576 8131
leckieandleckie@harpercollins.co.uk   www.leckieandleckie.co.uk

A CIP Catalogue record for this book is available from the British Library.

Questions and answers in this book do not emanate from SQA. All of our entirely new and original Practice Papers have been written by experienced authors working directly for the publisher.

Maps are reproduced by permission of Ordnance Survey on behalf of HMSO. © Crown Copyright 2010. All rights reserved.

Introduction

Layout of the book

This book contains practice exam papers which mirror the actual SQA exam as much as possible. The layout, paper colour and question level are all similar to those of the actual exam that you will sit, so that by the time you sit the exam, you will be familiar with what the exam paper looks like.

The answer section is at the back of the book. Each answer contains a worked-out answer or solution so that you can see how the right answer has been arrived at. The answers also include practical tips on how to tackle certain types of questions, details of how marks are awarded and advice on just what the examiners will be looking for.

Revision advice is provided in this introductory section of the book, so please read on!

How to use this book

The practice papers can be used in two main ways:

1. You can complete an entire practice paper as preparation for the final exam. If you would like to use the book in this way, you can either complete the practice paper under exam-style conditions by setting yourself a time limit for each paper and answering it as well as possible without using any references or notes or, alternatively, you can answer the practice paper questions as a revision exercise, using your notes to produce a model answer. Your teacher may mark these for you.

2. You can use the Topic Index at the front of this book to find all the questions within the book that deal with a specific topic. This allows you to focus specifically on areas that you particularly want to revise or, if you are mid-way through your course, it lets you practise answering exam-style questions for just those topics that you have studied.

Revision advice

Work out a revision timetable for each week's work in advance – remember to cover all of your subjects and to leave time for homework and breaks. For example:

Day	6pm–6.45pm	7pm–8pm	8.15pm–9pm	9.15pm–10pm
Monday	Homework	Homework	English revision	Chemistry revision
Tuesday	Maths revision	Geography revision	Homework	Free
Wednesday	Geography revision	Homework	English revision	Maths revision
Thursday	Homework	Geography revision	Chemistry revision	Free
Friday	Geography revision	Homework	Free	Free
Saturday	Free	Free	Free	Free
Sunday	Free	Maths revision	Chemistry revision	Homework

Make sure that you have at least one evening free a week to relax, socialise and re-charge your batteries. It also gives your brain a chance to process the information that you have been feeding it all week.

Arrange your study time into one-hour or 45-minute sessions, with a break between sessions, e.g. 6pm–6.45pm, 7pm–8pm, 8.15pm–9pm. Try to start studying as early as possible in the evening when your brain is still alert and be aware that the longer you put off starting, the harder it will be to start!

Study a different subject in each session, except for the day before an exam.

Do something different during your breaks between study sessions – have a cup of tea or listen to some music. Don't let your 15 minutes expand into 20 or 25 minutes, though!

Have your class notes and any textbooks available for your revision to hand as well as plenty of blank paper, a pen etc. You may like to make keyword sheets like the example below:

Keyword	Meaning
Secondary industry	Industries that manufacture things
Erosion	The process of wearing down the landscape

You may also like to practise drawing diagrams which may be included in your geography exam answers – for example, corries or pyramidal peaks.

Try to avoid cramming your studies on the night before the exam, or staying up late the night before the exam to study.

Finally, forget or ignore all or some of the advice in this section if you are happy with your present way of studying. Everyone revises differently, so find a way that works for you!

Transfer your knowledge

As well as using your class notes and textbooks to revise, these practice papers will also be a useful revision tool as they will help you to get used to answering exam-style questions. You may find as you work through the questions that they refer to a case study or an example that you haven't come across before. Don't worry! You should be able to transfer your knowledge of a topic or theme to a new example. The enhanced answer section at the back will demonstrate how to read and interpret the question to identify the topic being examined and how to apply your course knowledge in order to answer the question successfully.

Command words

In the practice paper questions, and in the exam itself, a number of command words will be used. These command words are used to show you how you should answer a question, and some words indicate that you should write more than others. If you familiarise yourself with these command words, it will help you to structure your answers more effectively.

Command Word	Meaning/Explanation
Suggest	Give more than a list – perhaps a proposal or an idea.
Outline	Give a brief description or overview of what you are talking about.
Describe	Give more detail than you would in an outline, and use examples where you can.
Explain	Discuss why an action has been taken or an outcome reached – what are the reasons and/or processes behind it?
Justify	Give reasons for your answer, stating why you have taken an action or reached a particular conclusion.
Define	Give the meaning of the term.
Compare	Give the key features of two different items or ideas and discuss their similarities and/or their differences.

Structure of the exam

There are two question papers for Higher Geography, each marked out of 100.

The time allocation for Paper 1 is 1 hour 30 minutes, and it consists of three sections, A, B and C. Section A contains four compulsory questions – two on topics on the Physical Environment and two on the Human Environment. Section B has questions on the two Physical Environment topics not examined in section A, of which you have to answer one. Section C has questions on the two Human Environment topics not examined in section A, of which you also have to answer one.

The time allocation for Paper 2 is 1 hour 15 minutes. It covers Environmental Interactions and contains six questions. You must answer any two of these questions, and each question is worth 50 marks.

Topic	Exam 1	Exam 2	Exam 3	Knowledge for prelim			Knowledge for SQA exam		
				Have difficulty	Still needs work	OK	Have difficulty	Still needs work	OK
Urban change and its management									
Growth of developing world cities	4a								
Shanty town problems	4bi								
Tackling shanty town problems	4bii								
Urban fringe – developed world cities	4ci								
Conflicts in urban fringe	4cii								
Strategies to solve the conflicts	4cii								
Population growth in developing world cities		4a							
Problems of growth in developing world cities		4bi							
Solutions to problems caused by rapid growth in the developed world		4bii							
Effectiveness of solutions		4biii							
Problems in developed world cities		4ci							
Solving problems in developed world cities		4cii							
Site and situation in growth of developed world cities			4a						
Redevelopment areas in developed world cities			4bi						
Changes and their usefulness in developed world cities			4bii						
Success of methods used		4ciii							
Different growth in developed and developing world cities			4c						
Problems in shanty towns			4d						

Topic	Exam 1	Exam 2	Exam 3	Knowledge for prelim			Knowledge for SQA exam		
				Have difficulty	Still needs work	OK	Have difficulty	Still needs work	OK
Development and health									
Variation in levels of development in developing world countries	5a								
Primary health care	5b								
Physical and human causes of spread of a selected disease	5ci								
Measures to combat chosen disease	5cii								
Effectiveness of measures	5ciii								
Development indicators		5a							
Differences in development levels between developing countries		5b	5b						
Differences in development within a developing country		5c							
Human and environmental conditions contributing to spread of chosen disease		5di							
Measures used to control spread of chosen disease		5dii							
Success of methods to control spread of disease		5diii							
PQLI and HDI			5a						
Primary health care's contribution to development			5c						
Measures to combat selected water-related disease			5di						
How disease hinders development			5dii						

Exam 1

Examination advice

Give yourself plenty of time by arriving early for the exam, well equipped with pens, pencils, rulers etc.

Be clear before the exam what the instructions are likely to be, for example how many questions you should answer in each section. The practice papers will help you to become familiar with the exam instructions.

Read each question thoroughly before you begin to answer it. Make sure you know exactly what the question is asking you to do. If the question is in sections, for example 15a, 15b, 15c etc, make sure that you can answer each section before you start writing.

Plan your answer by jotting down keywords, a mindmap or reminders of the important things to include in your answer. Cross them off as you deal with them and check before you move on to the next question that you haven't forgotten anything.

Note that when writing your answer, it must be in essay form with proper paragraphs. You should avoid giving answers in note-like form or using bullet points.

Give proper explanations. A common error is to give descriptions rather than explanations. If you are asked to explain something, you must give reasons. Make sure your answer to an 'explain' question has plenty of linking words and phrases such as 'because', 'this means that', 'therefore', 'so', 'so that', 'due to', 'since' and 'the reason is'.

Use the resources provided. Some questions will ask you to 'describe and explain', and provide an example or a case study for you to work from. Make sure that you take any relevant data from these resources.

Watch your time and pace yourself carefully. Work out roughly how much time you can spend on each answer and try to stick to this.

If you have any time left over in the exam, use this time productively by going back over your answers and perhaps providing additional parts to your answer. This is especially helpful in Ordnance Survey map-based questions.

Common errors to avoid

Markers of the external examination often remark on errors which occur frequently in candidates' answers. These include the following:

1. Use grid references

In questions that ask for evidence from Ordnance Survey maps, your answer should include grid references, preferably 6-figure grid references.

2. Use diagrams

If a question says 'with the aid of diagrams', you may lose marks if your answer doesn't include diagrams. Full marks can be gained for fully-annotated diagrams.

3. Lack of sufficient detail

This often occurs in Higher case study answers, especially in 10 to 18 mark questions. Many candidates fail to provide sufficient detail, often by omitting reference to specific examples, or not elaborating or developing points made in their answer. A good guide to the amount of detail required is the number of marks given for the question. If, for example, the question is worth a total of 10 marks, then you should make at least six valid points for a pass.

4. Listing

If you give a simple list of points rather than fuller statements in your answer you may lose marks; for example, in a 4 mark question, you will obtain only 1 mark for a list.

The same rule applies to a simple list of bullet points.

5. Irrelevant answers

You must read the question instructions carefully so as to avoid giving answers which are irrelevant. For example, if asked to explain and you simply describe, you will not score marks. If asked for a named example and you do not provide one, you will forfeit marks.

6. Reversals

Occasionally questions involve opposites. For example, your answer to a question might say: 'Death rates are high in developing countries due to poor health care'. Don't then go on to say 'Death rates are low in developed countries due to good health care'. You would simply be stating the reverse of the first statement. A better second statement might be that 'high standards of hygiene, health and education in developed countries have helped to bring about low death rates'.

7. Lack of specific detail

Avoid vague answers when asked for detail. Avoid general terms such as 'dry soils' or 'fertile soils' if you can give more detailed information, e.g. 'deep and well-drained soils' or 'rich in nutrients'.

If you are asked for a named country or city, make sure you include details of any case study you have covered.

If you are given data in the form of maps, diagrams and tables in the question, make sure you use this information in your answer to support any points of view you give. If describing climates, give climate figures.

Topic Index: Paper 1

Topic	Exam 1	Exam 2	Exam 3	Knowledge for prelim			Knowledge for SQA exam		
				Have difficulty	Still needs work	OK	Have difficulty	Still needs work	OK
Atmosphere									
Solar energy	5a								
Global mean temperatures	5b								
Air masses		1a							
ITCZ		1b							
Circulation cells			5a						
Ocean currents			5b						
Hydrosphere									
River courses on OS maps	1a								
Oxbow lakes	1b								
River characteristics on OS maps		5a							
Waterfall formation		5b							
Hydrological cycle			6a						
Rural and urban hydrographs			6b						
Lithosphere									
Features of carboniferous limestone	6								
Features of glacial erosion on OS maps		2a							
Formation of glacial features		2b							
Formation of coastal features			1a						
Slumping			1b						

Practice Papers for SQA Exams: Higher Geography

Topic	Exam 1	Exam 2	Exam 3	Knowledge for prelim			Knowledge for SQA exam		
				Have difficulty	Still needs work	OK	Have difficulty	Still needs work	OK
Biosphere									
Plant succession	2a								
Psamoseres	2b								
Soil profiles		6a							
Soil formation		6b							
Changes in plant life moving inland from coast			2a						
Colonisation of sand dunes			2b						
Population geography									
Population structures	3a								
Reasons for changing population structures	3b								
Migration push/pull patterns		7a							
Advantages and disadvantages to receiving country		7b							
Collection of census data in a developed country			3a						
Reliability of census data			3b						
Rural geography									
Shifting cultivation and commercial arable farming	7a								
Intensive peasant farming		3a							
Impact of recent changes on the people/environment in areas of shifting cultivation or commercial arable farming	7b								
How changes in intensive peasant farming affect the environment and local people		3b							
Farming systems			7a						
Impact of change in farming systems on environment and people			7b						

Page 8

Practice Papers for SQA Exams: Higher Geography

Topic	Exam 1	Exam 2	Exam 3	Knowledge for prelim			Knowledge for SQA exam		
				Have difficulty	Still needs work	OK	Have difficulty	Still needs work	OK
Industrial geography									
Location factors for original industry		4a							
Factors leading to industrial decline		4b							
Factors affecting growth of traditional industry			4a						
Impact of human and economic factors on location of new industry			4b						
Location factors relating to car industry	8								
Urban geography									
Describing and explaining differences in two residential areas on an OS map			8a						
Explaining site factors for a shopping centre based on OS map evidence			8b						
Land use in developed world city zones	4a								
Out of town shopping centres	4b								
Site and situation factors in a developed world city		8a							
Changes in the CBD of a developed world city		8b							

Topic Index: Paper 2

Topic	Exam 1	Exam 2	Exam 3	Knowledge for prelim			Knowledge for SQA exam		
				Have difficulty	Still needs work	OK	Have difficulty	Still needs work	OK
Rural land resources									
Coastal features (formation processes)	1a								
Economic and social opportunities in named coastal area created by landscape	1b								
Environmental problems and conflicts in coastal areas created by competing land uses	1ci								
Measures taken to resolve environmental conflicts in coastal areas	1cii								
Social and economic opportunities provided by landscape in a named National Park		1a							
Features of carboniferous limestone		1b							
Popularity of National Parks		1ci	1a						
Benefits of visitors to National Parks related to tourism		1cii							
Tourist problems and measures taken to tackle them		1ciii							
Environmental problems in National Parks with glaciated scenery			1bi						
Tackling environmental problems and success of measures taken			1bii						
Formation of glaciated features			1c						

Practice Papers for SQA Exams: Higher Geography

Topic	Exam 1	Exam 2	Exam 3	Knowledge for prelim			Knowledge for SQA exam		
				Have difficulty	Still needs work	OK	Have difficulty	Still needs work	OK
Rural land degradation									
Wind and water erosion	2a								
Human causes of rural land degradation	2b								
Impact of rural land degradation on humans	2c								
Methods used to prevent soil erosion	2di								
Effectiveness of methods used to prevent soil erosion	2dii								
Effects of changing rainfall patterns in the Sahel Zone, Africa		2a							
Factors leading to rural land degradation		2bi							
Impact of land degradation on people and the environment		2bii							
Soil conservation methods		2c							
Wind erosion processes			2a						
Contribution of physical and human factors to rural land degradation			2b						
Measures to prevent soil erosion			2ci						
Soil conservation methods in rural areas			2cii						
Inappropriate farming techniques			2d						

Page 11

Practice Papers for SQA Exams: Higher Geography

Topic	Exam 1	Exam 2	Exam 3	Knowledge for prelim			Knowledge for SQA exam		
				Have difficulty	Still needs work	OK	Have difficulty	Still needs work	OK
River basin management									
Need for water management	3a								
Selection of a site for a dam	3b								
Benefits/adverse consequences of water management project	3c								
Political problems created by water projects	3d								
Effect of water management schemes on hydrological cycle		3a							
Physical and human factors affecting site of a dam		3b							
Benefits/problems of water management projects		3c							
Political problems of river running through more than one state or country		3d							
Distribution of river basins			3a						
Need for water management in Egypt			3b						
Benefits of water management in Nile Basin			3c						
Political conflicts resulting from river control schemes			3d						

Higher Geography

Practice Papers
For SQA Exams

Time allowed:
1 hour, 30 minutes

Exam 1, Paper 1

You should attempt **six** questions:

- **every** question in **Section A** (Questions 1, 2, 3 and 4);
- **one** question in **Section B** (Question 5 **or** Question 6);
- **one** question in **Section C** (Question 7 **or** Question 8).

The marks available for each question are shown in the margin.

Marks will be given for suitable maps and diagrams, and for reference to named examples.

Write your answers in sentences.

Note   The reference maps and diagrams in this paper have been printed in black only: no other colours have been used.

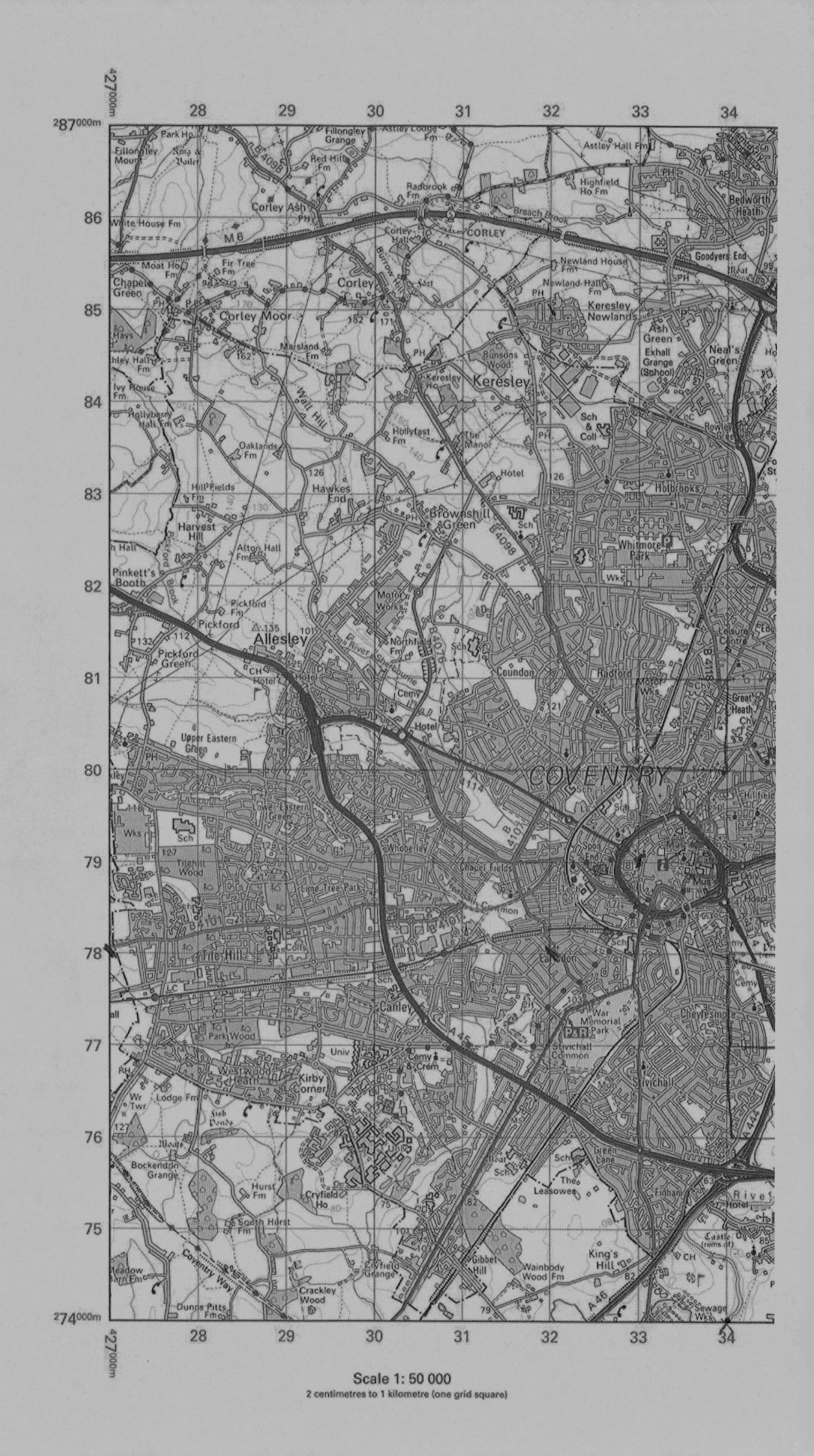

Scale 1: 50 000
2 centimetres to 1 kilometre (one grid square)

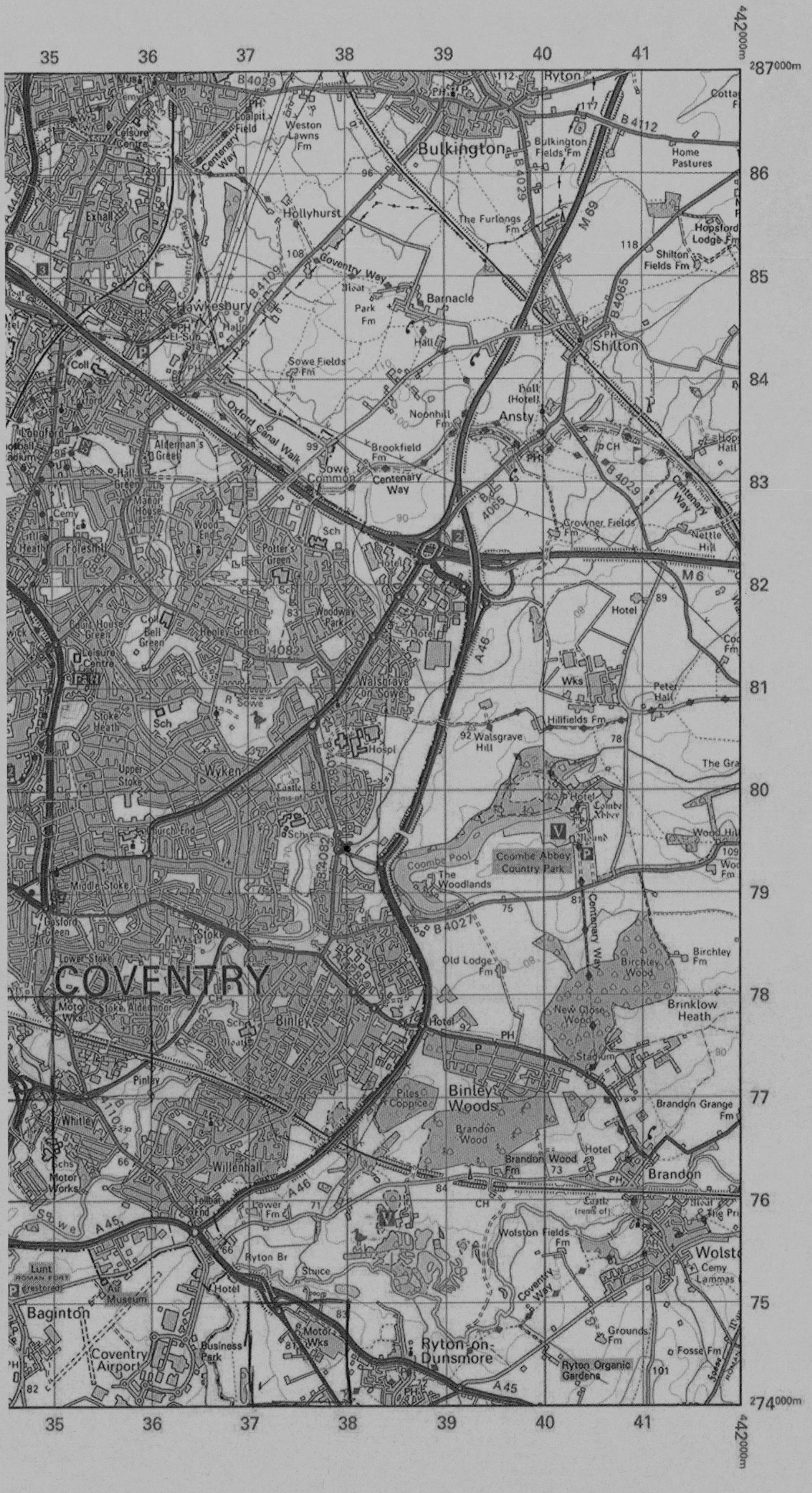

35
36
37
38
39
40
41
442000m
287000m
86
85
84
83
82
81
80
79
78
77
76
75
274000m
Ryton
B 4029
B 4112
Coalpit Field
Weston Lawns Fm
Leisure Centre
Centenary Way
Bulkington
Bulkington Fields Fm
Home Pastures
Exhall
Hollyhurst
The Furlongs Fm
M 69
Hopsford Lodge Fm
Shilton Fields Fm
118
108
Coventry Way
B 4109
Barnacle
Park Fm
Hawkesbury
B 4065
Shilton
Hall
Sowe Fields Fm
Coll
Hall (Hotel)
Noonhill Fm
Ansty
Longford
Oxford Canal Walk
Alderman's Green
Brookfield Fm
CH
Sowe Common
Centenary Way
Hall Green
Manor House
B 4029
Cemy
Wood End
Little Heath
Foleshill
Sch
Potter's Green
Crowner Fields Fm
Nettle Hill
M 6
Hotel
Court House Green
Bell Green
Henley Green
Woodway Park
B 4082
A 46
Leisure Centre
89
Wks
R Sowe
Walsgrave on Sowe
Peter Hall
Stoke Heath
Sch
Hillfields Fm
Hospl
92 Walsgrave Hill
78
Upper Stoke
Wyken
Hotel
Combe Abbey
Church End
Coombe Pool
Coombe Abbey Country Park
The Woodlands
Middle Stoke
B 4027
75
Centenary Way
Gosford Green
Stoke
Lower Stoke
Old Lodge Fm
Birchley Wood
Birchley Fm
COVENTRY
Motor Wks
Stoke Aldermoor
Binley
Hotel
PH
New Close Wood
Brinklow Heath
Stadium
Pinley
Piles Coppice
Binley Woods
Brandon Grange Fm
Whitley
Brandon Wood
Hotel
Brandon Wood Fm
73
Schs
Motor Works
Willenhall
84
Brandon
Tollbar End
A 46
Lower Fm
71
CH
A 45
Wolston Fields Fm
Lunt ROMAN FORT (restored)
Ryton Br
Sluice
Coventry Way
Cemy
Air Museum
Hotel
Baginton
Business Park
Motor Wks
83
Grounds Fm
Coventry Airport
Ryton-on-Dunsmore
Fosse Fm
Ryton Organic Gardens
101
82
A 45

SECTION A

Answer all the questions in this section

QUESTION 1: Hydrosphere

Study the Ordnance Survey Map Extract number 1742/140: Coventry.

(*a*) Examine the course of the River Sowe between 380795 and 340740.

Using appropriate grid references, **describe** the physical characteristics of the River Sowe and its valley. **10**

(*b*) Oxbow lakes are common features in the lower course of a river.

Explain, with the aid of a diagram or diagrams, how an oxbow lake is formed. **8**

Diagram Q1: Oxbow lakes

QUESTION 2: Biosphere

(a) **Describe** and **explain** the process of plant succession. **6**

(b) Study Diagram Q2.

Describe and **explain** the changes in plant species to be found at sites 1–4 on the transect below. (Your answer should refer to specific plant types.) **12**

Diagram Q2: Sand dune transect

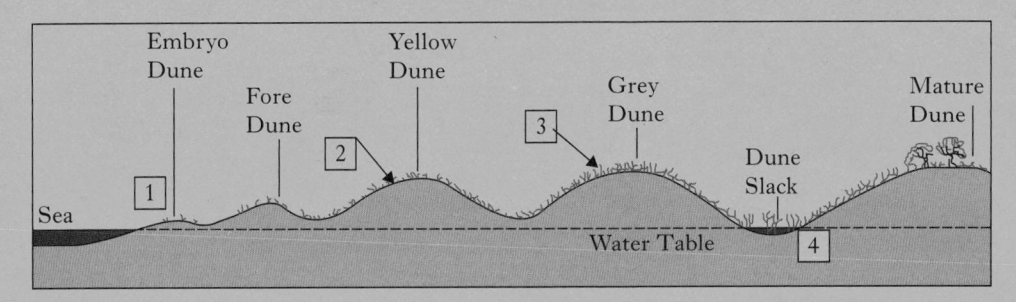

QUESTION 3: Population

Study Diagrams Q3A and Q3B.

Malawi is a developing country.

(a) **Describe** and **explain** the population structure for 2009. **10**

(b) **Describe** the predicted population structure in 2029 and suggest reasons for the predicted changes. **8**

Diagram Q3A: Population pyramid for Malawi in 2009

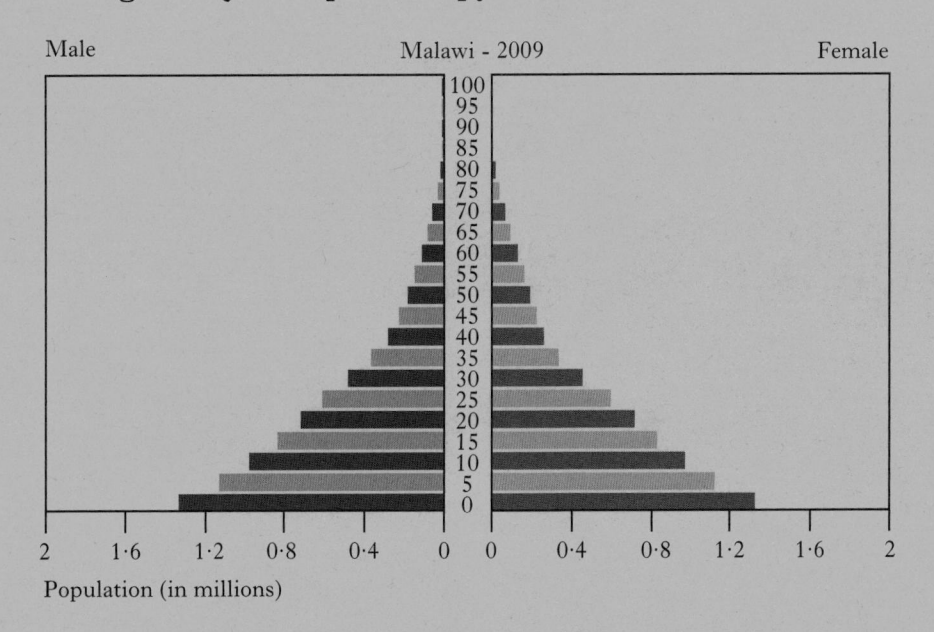

QUESTION 3 : continued

Diagram Q3B: Predicted population pyramid for Malawi 2029

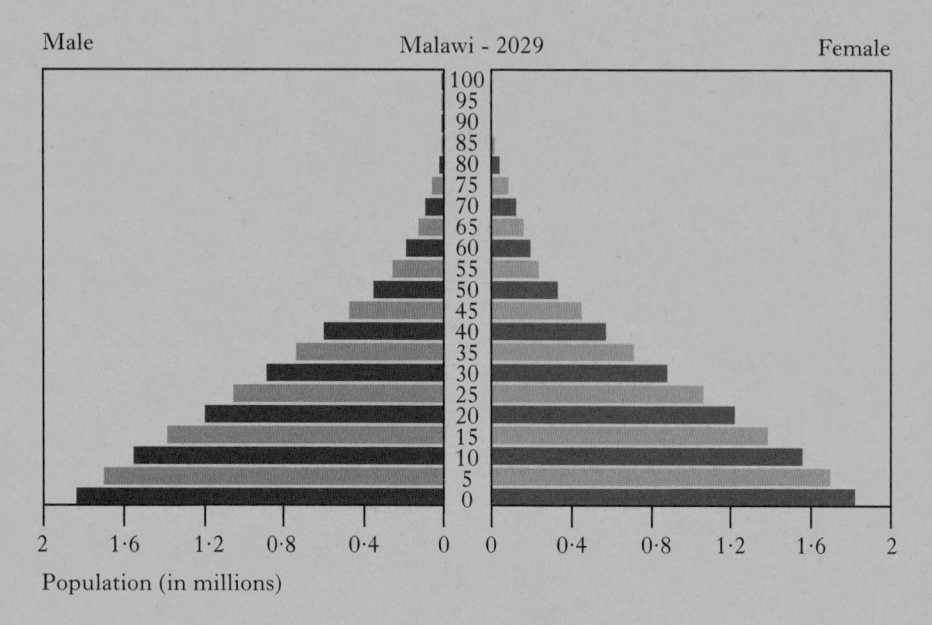

QUESTION 4: Urban Geography

With reference to a city you have studied in the developed world:

(a) Study Diagram Q4.

Describe and give reasons for the likely land uses which would be found in Zone A of your chosen city. **10**

(b) **Explain** how an out of town shopping centre could have an impact on the shops in the Central Business District (CBD). **8**

Diagram Q4: Land use zones in a city

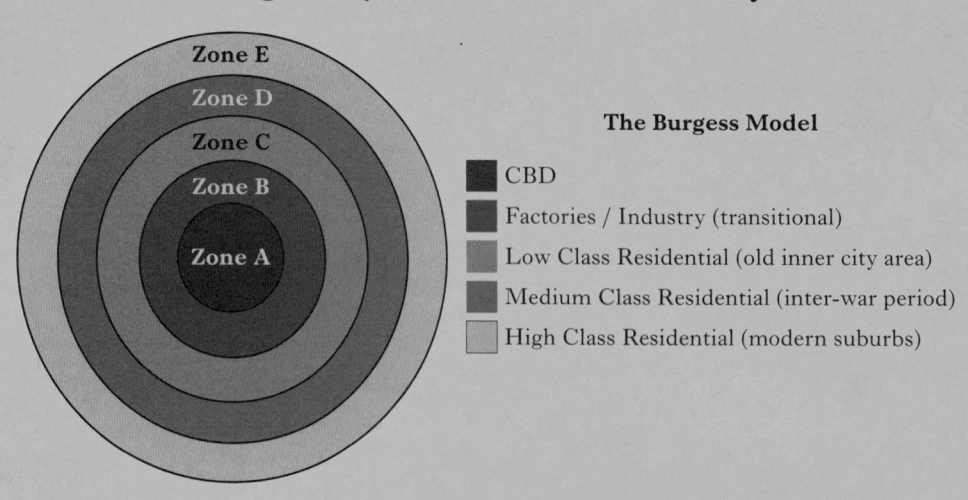

The Burgess Model
- CBD
- Factories / Industry (transitional)
- Low Class Residential (old inner city area)
- Medium Class Residential (inter-war period)
- High Class Residential (modern suburbs)

SECTION B

**Answer ONE question from this section,
i.e. either Question 5 or Question 6**

QUESTION 5: Atmosphere

(a) Using an annotated diagram or diagrams, **explain** why there is a net gain of solar energy in tropical latitudes and a net loss towards the poles. **8**

(b) Study Diagram Q5.

   Explain the physical factors which may have led to the changes in global mean temperatures shown in Diagram Q5. **6**

Diagram Q5: Changes in global mean temperatures 1860 to 2000

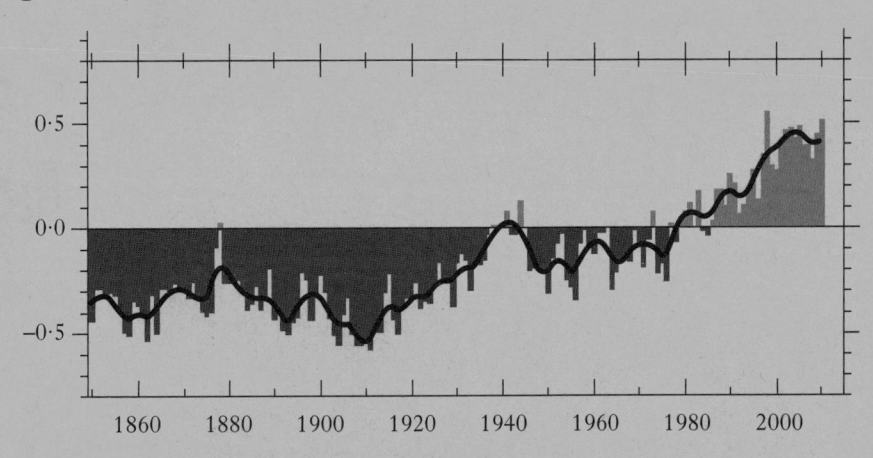

DO NOT ANSWER THIS QUESTION IF YOU HAVE ALREADY ANSWERED QUESTION 5

QUESTION 6: Lithosphere

Study Diagram Q6.

Choose **two** of the features of carboniferous limestone from the list below and **explain**, with the aid of a diagram or diagrams, the processes involved in their formation:

(i) swallow hole

(ii) limestone pavement

(iii) stalactites **and** stalagmites **14**

Diagram Q6: A carboniferous limestone landscape

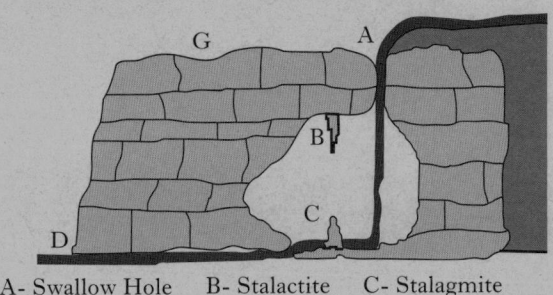

A- Swallow Hole   B- Stalactite   C- Stalagmite
D- Resurgence   G- Limestone Pavement

SECTION C

**Answer ONE question from this section,
i.e. either Question 7 or Question 8**

QUESTION 7: Rural Geography

Study Diagrams Q7A and Q7B, which show two different farming systems.

(a) For **either** shifting cultivation **or** commercial arable farming, **describe** the main characteristics of the farming system. **8**

(b) With reference to a named area of shifting cultivation **or** commercial arable farming, explain the impact of recent changes on the local people and the environment. **6**

Diagram Q7A: Shifting cultivation

Diagram Q7B: Commercial arable farming

DO NOT ANSWER THIS QUESTION IF YOU HAVE
ALREADY ANSWERED QUESTION 7

Marks

QUESTION 8: Industrial Geography

Study the Ordnance Survey Map Extract number 1742/140: Coventry and Diagrams Q8A and Q8B.

There are several motor works in Coventry.

Explain, using map evidence and Diagrams Q8A and Q8B, why Coventry is a good location for the motor car industry.

14

Diagram Q8A: Location of Coventry in the UK

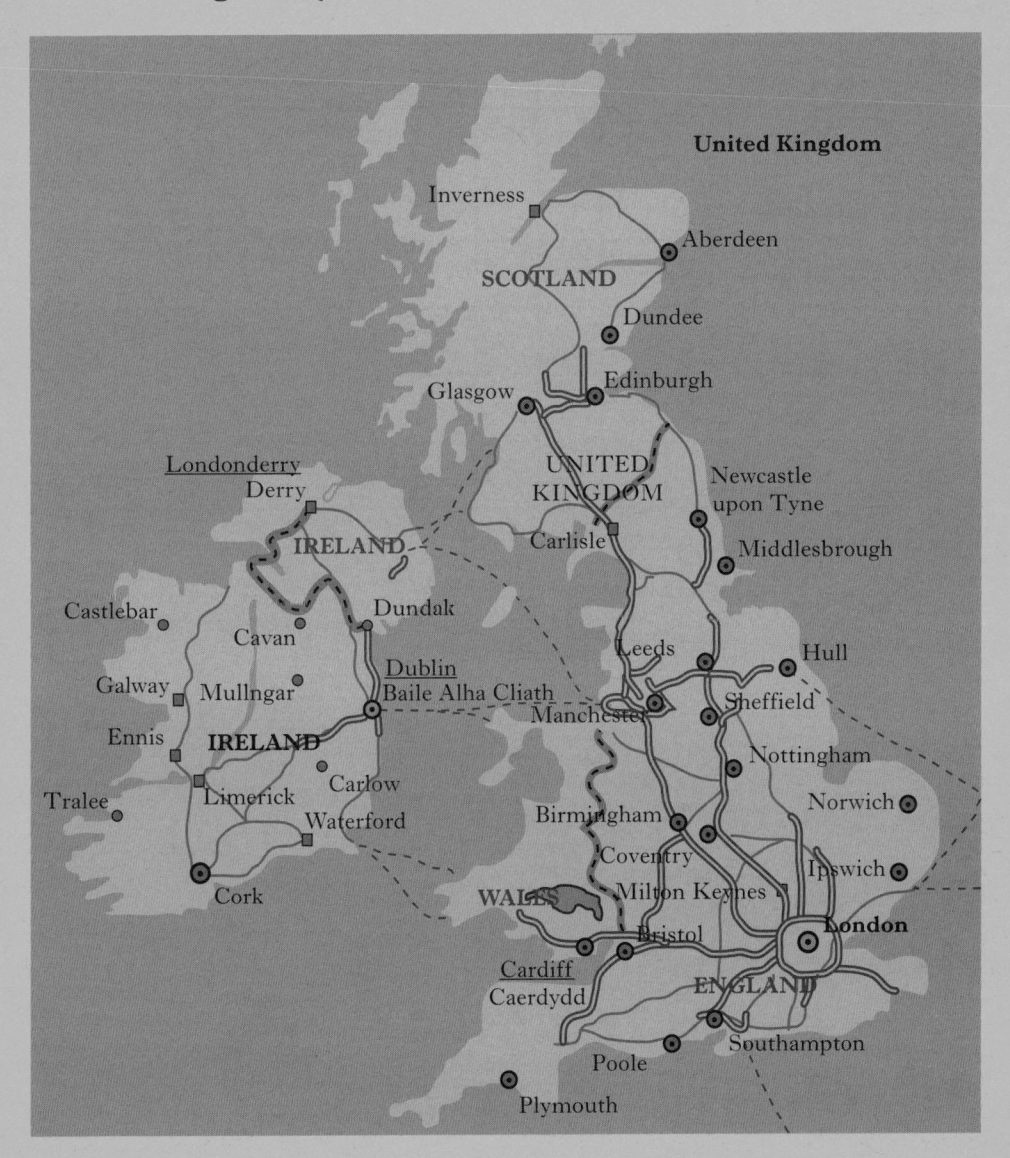

QUESTION 8: continued

Diagram Q8B: Location of motor works in Coventry

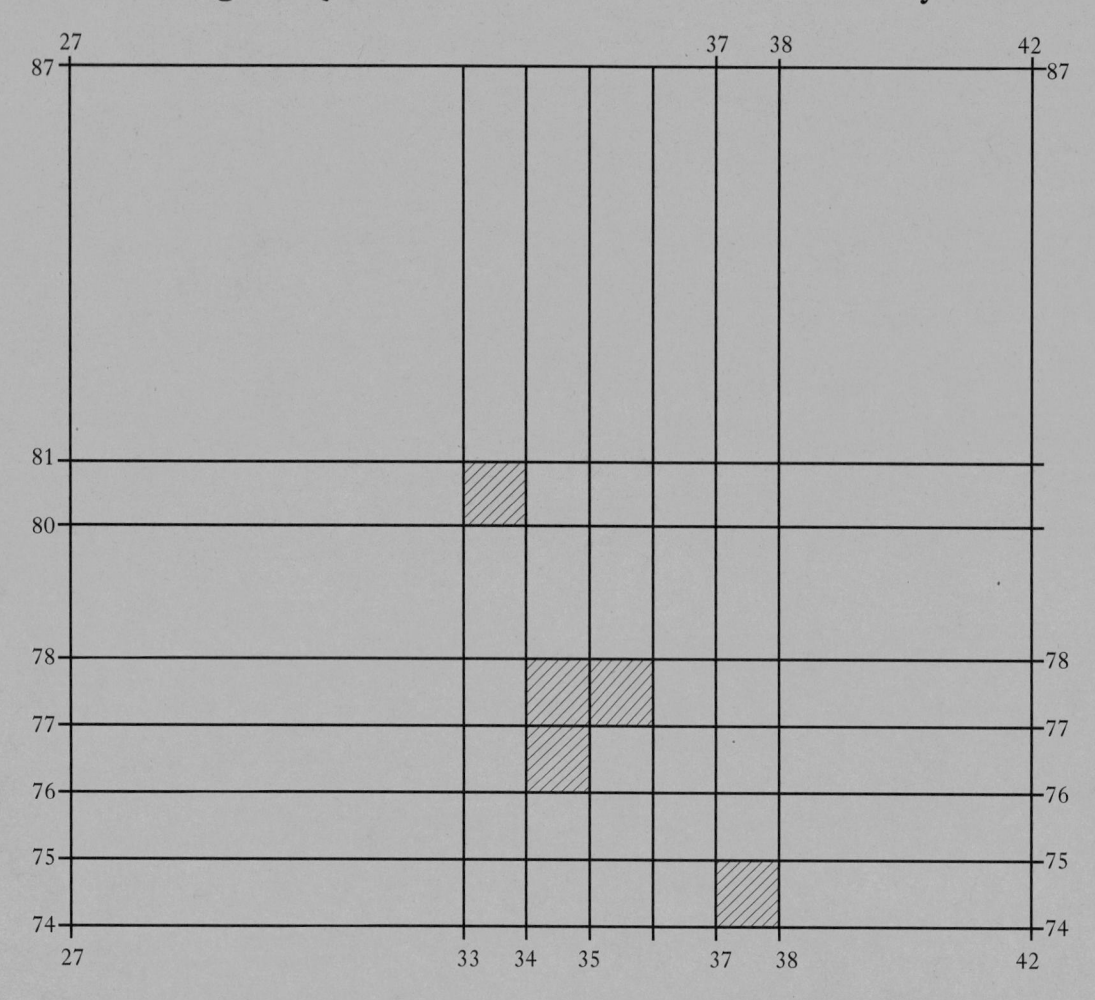

[End of question paper]

Higher Geography

Practice Papers
For SQA Exams

Time allowed:
1 hour, 15 minutes

Exam 1, Paper 2

You should attempt **two** questions.

The marks available for each question are shown in the margin.

Marks will be given for suitable maps and diagrams, and for reference to named examples.

Write your answers in sentences.

Note   The reference maps and diagrams in this paper have been printed in black only: no other colours have been used.

QUESTION 1: Rural Land Resources

Marks

(a) Look at Diagram Q1A.

With the aid of annotated diagrams, **describe** and **explain** the main features of any coastal landscape which you have studied.

Your answer should refer to both erosional and depositional features. **20**

(b) With reference to any named coastal area you have studied, **describe** the economic and social opportunities created by the landscape. **8**

(c) Look at Diagram Q1B (Tourist Map of Studland, Dorset).

'This coast is a designated World Heritage Coast and an Area of Outstanding Beauty. On summer days and holidays the Studland area can receive up to 20 000 visitors taking part in a wide variety of activities.'

For Studland or any other named coastal area you have studied,

(i) **Describe** and **explain** the environmental problems and conflicts which may arise from competing land uses. **14**

(ii) **Describe** the measures taken to resolve environmental conflicts related to tourism. **8**

(50)

Diagram Q1A: Selected features of the Jurassic Coast

Diagram Q1B: Land use around Purbeck, Dorset

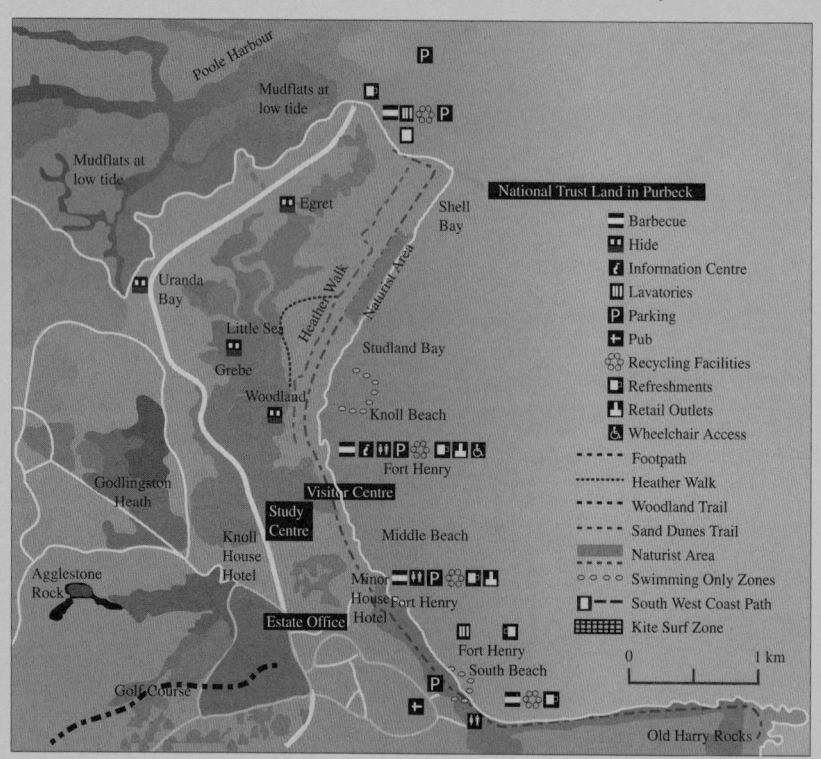

QUESTION 2: Rural Land Degradation

Marks

(a) **Describe** and **explain** the processes of **either** wind **or** water erosion. **8**

(b) The United Nations Convention to Combat Desertification defines desertification as 'Land degradation in arid, semi arid and dry sub-humid areas resulting from various factors including climatic variations and human activities'.

Describe and **explain** the human causes that can lead to rural land degradation in either North America, the Amazon Basin or Africa, north of the equator. **16**

(c) Look at Diagram Q2.

Referring to named locations in either North America or Africa north of the equator, **explain** how land degradation affects the way of life in that area. **10**

(d) 'The Dust Bowl taught farmers new farming methods and techniques but perhaps the most valuable lesson learned from the Dust Bowl was the need to take care of the land.' (Quote from government official.)

For named areas you have studied in North America:

(i) **Describe** and **explain** the methods used by farmers to prevent soil erosion and reduce land degradation.

(ii) How effective have these measures been? **16**

(50)

Diagram Q2: Current state of desertification

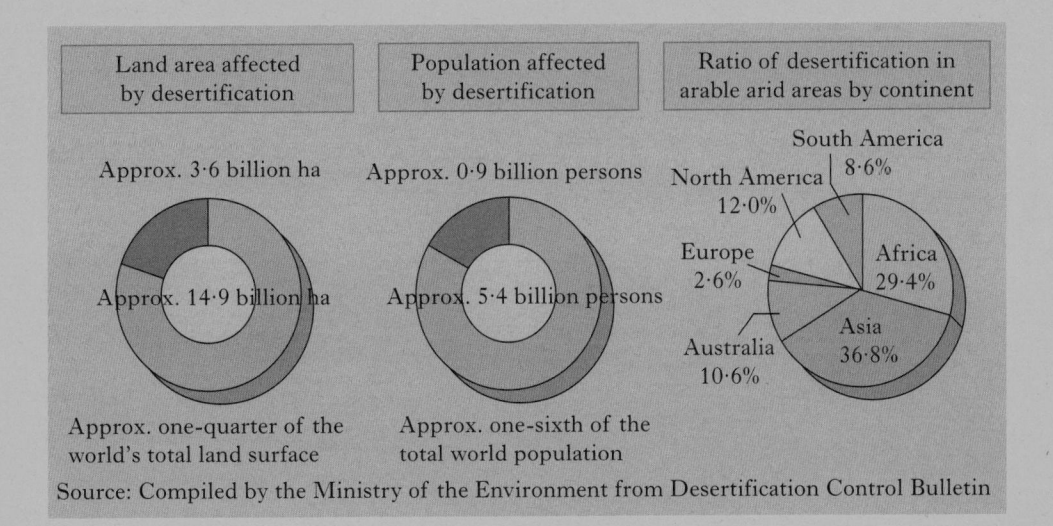

Land area affected by desertification	Population affected by desertification	Ratio of desertification in arable arid areas by continent
Approx. 3·6 billion ha / Approx. 14·9 billion ha	Approx. 0·9 billion persons / Approx. 5·4 billion persons	South America 8·6%, North America 12·0%, Europe 2·6%, Africa 29·4%, Asia 36·8%, Australia 10·6%
Approx. one-quarter of the world's total land surface	Approx. one-sixth of the total world population	

Source: Compiled by the Ministry of the Environment from Desertification Control Bulletin

QUESTION 3: River Basin Management

Study Maps Q3A and Q3B, and Diagram Q3C.

(a) **Explain** why there is a need for water management in the Damodar Valley, India. **10**

(b) For the Panchet Dam or any other dam you have studied in Asia, Africa or North America, **explain** the physical factors which have to be taken into consideration when selecting the site for the dam. **10**

QUESTION 3: continued

Marks

(c) For your chosen water management project, **describe** and **explain** the social, economic and environmental benefits and adverse consequences of the project.

24

(d) The Nile and the Colorado rivers are examples of rivers which flow through more than one country. For any water project you have studied in Asia, Africa or North America, **explain** the political problems which may have resulted from the project.

6

(50)

Map Q3A: Map of the Damodar Valley, India

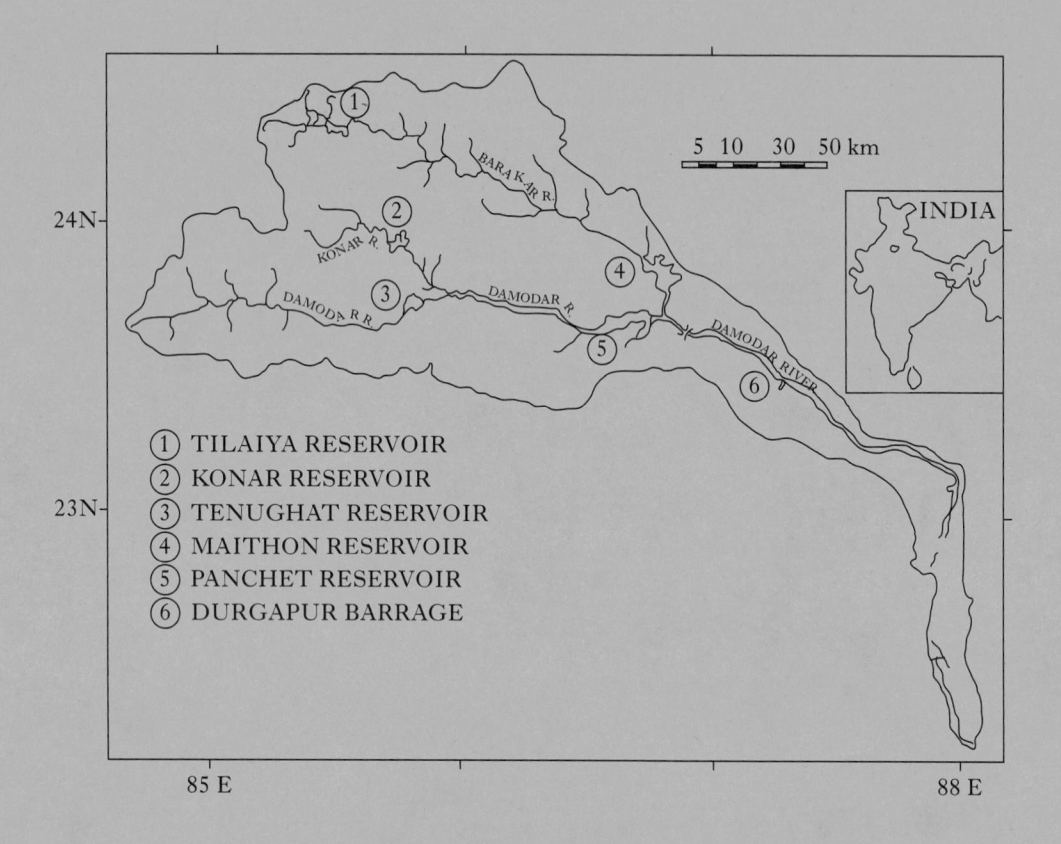

① TILAIYA RESERVOIR
② KONAR RESERVOIR
③ TENUGHAT RESERVOIR
④ MAITHON RESERVOIR
⑤ PANCHET RESERVOIR
⑥ DURGAPUR BARRAGE

QUESTION 3: continued

Map Q3B: Flood zones, India

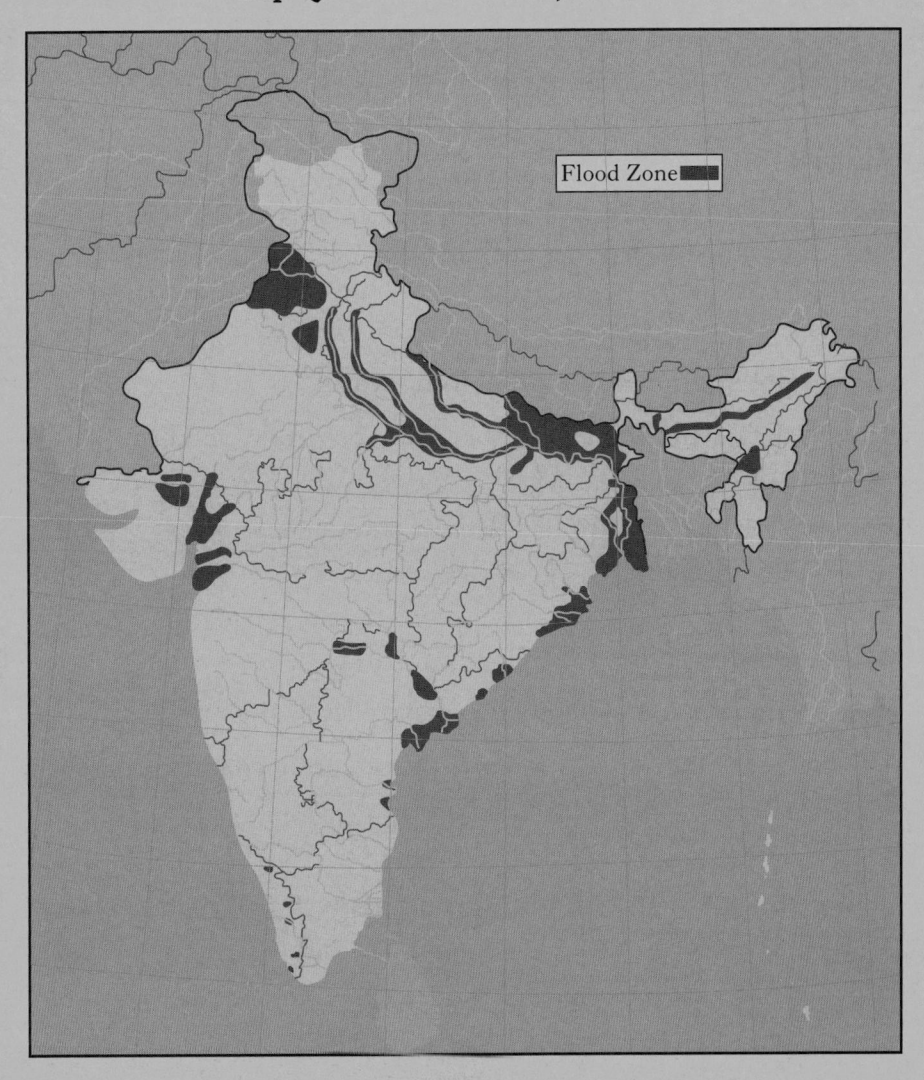

Diagram Q3C: Climate graph of Panchet, India

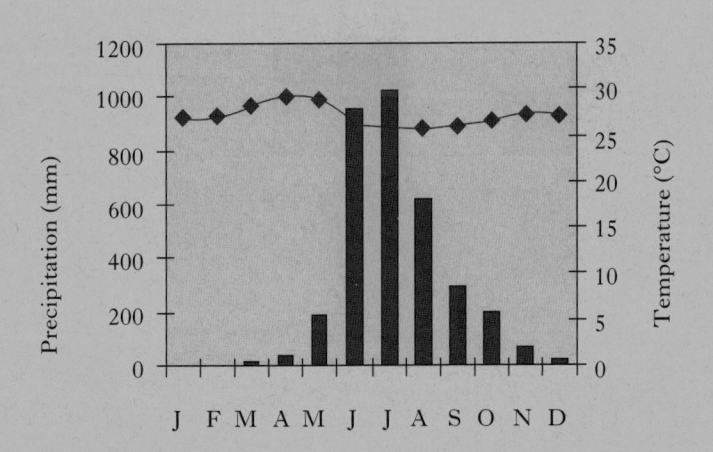

QUESTION 4: Urban Change and its Management

(a) Look at Diagram Q4A.

Referring to named cities you have studied, suggest reasons why the populations of developing world cities grow much faster than those of developed world cities. **12**

(b) Look at Diagram Q4B.

'A shanty town is a group of unplanned shelters constructed from cheap or waste materials (such as cardboard, wood and cloth). Shanty towns are commonly located on the outskirts of cities in poor countries, or within large cities on derelict land or near rubbish tips.'

For any city you have studied in the developing world,

(i) **describe**, in detail, the economic, social and environmental problems created by shanty towns; and

(ii) **describe** possible methods to tackle these problems. **18**

(c) Study Diagram Q4C.

Referring to London or any other developed world city,

(i) give reasons why land use conflicts may have occurred on the urban fringe; and

(ii) **describe** some strategies used to solve these conflicts and comment on their effectiveness. **20**

(50)

Diagram Q4A: Urban population growth (billions)

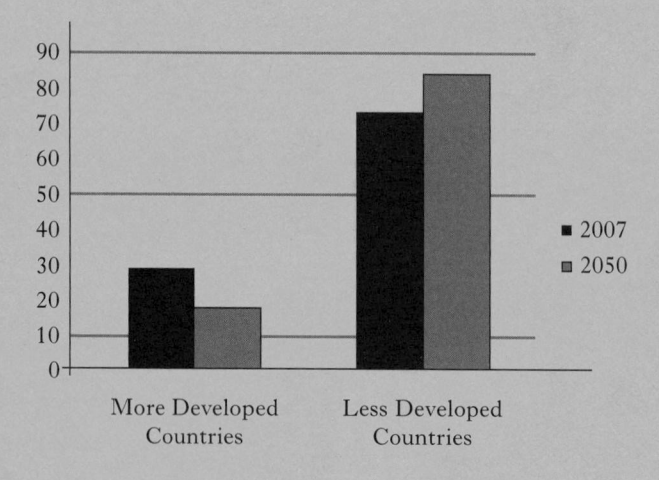

Practice Papers for SQA Exams: Higher Geography, Practice Exam 1, Paper 2

Marks

QUESTION 4: continued

Diagram Q4B: A Shanty town

Diagram Q4C: Part of London's urban-rural fringe

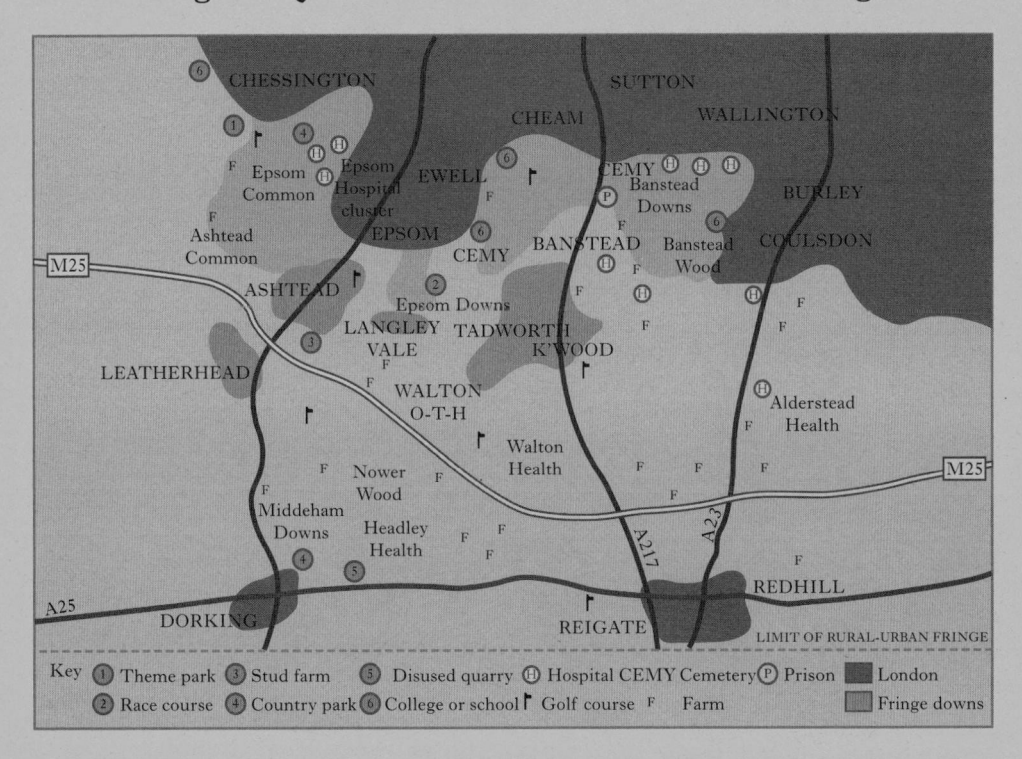

QUESTION 5: Development and Health

Marks

(a) Diagram Q5A below shows data for three countries in the developing world.

For these countries, or similar countries you have studied, suggest reasons for the different levels of development between the countries.

10

Diagram Q5A: Population statistics for selected countries

Country	GDP per capita (US $)	Infant mortality/1000	Life expectancy (years)
Sierra Leone	700	154	37
India	2780	57	63
South Korea	25 800	4	78

(b) Basic health care in a developing country can be provided through a Primary Health Care (PHC) programme.

For a named country you have studied, **describe** examples of Primary Health Care strategies and **explain** how they can improve the health of the people.

10

(c) Diagram Q5B shows areas of the world where malaria can be found.

For malaria, or cholera, **or** bilharzia:

(i) **describe** the physical and human conditions required for people to catch the disease;

(ii) **describe** measures used to combat the disease;

(iii) for the measures you have described in part (ii) **evaluate** how successful they have been.

30

(50)

Diagram Q5B: Areas at risk from Malaria

● Malaria risk
○ No malaria

[End of question paper]

Higher Geography

| Practice Papers
For SQA Exams | Time allowed:
1 hour, 30 minutes | Exam 2, Paper 1 |

You should attempt **six** questions:

- **every** question in **Section A** (Questions 1, 2, 3 and 4);
- **one** question in **Section B** (Question 5 **or** Question 6);
- **one** question in **Section C** (Question 7 **or** Question 8).

The marks available for each question are shown in the margin.

Marks will be given for suitable maps and diagrams, and for reference to named examples.

Write your answers in sentences.

Note The reference maps and diagrams in this paper have been printed in black only: no other colours have been used.

1:50 000 Scale
Landranger Series

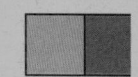

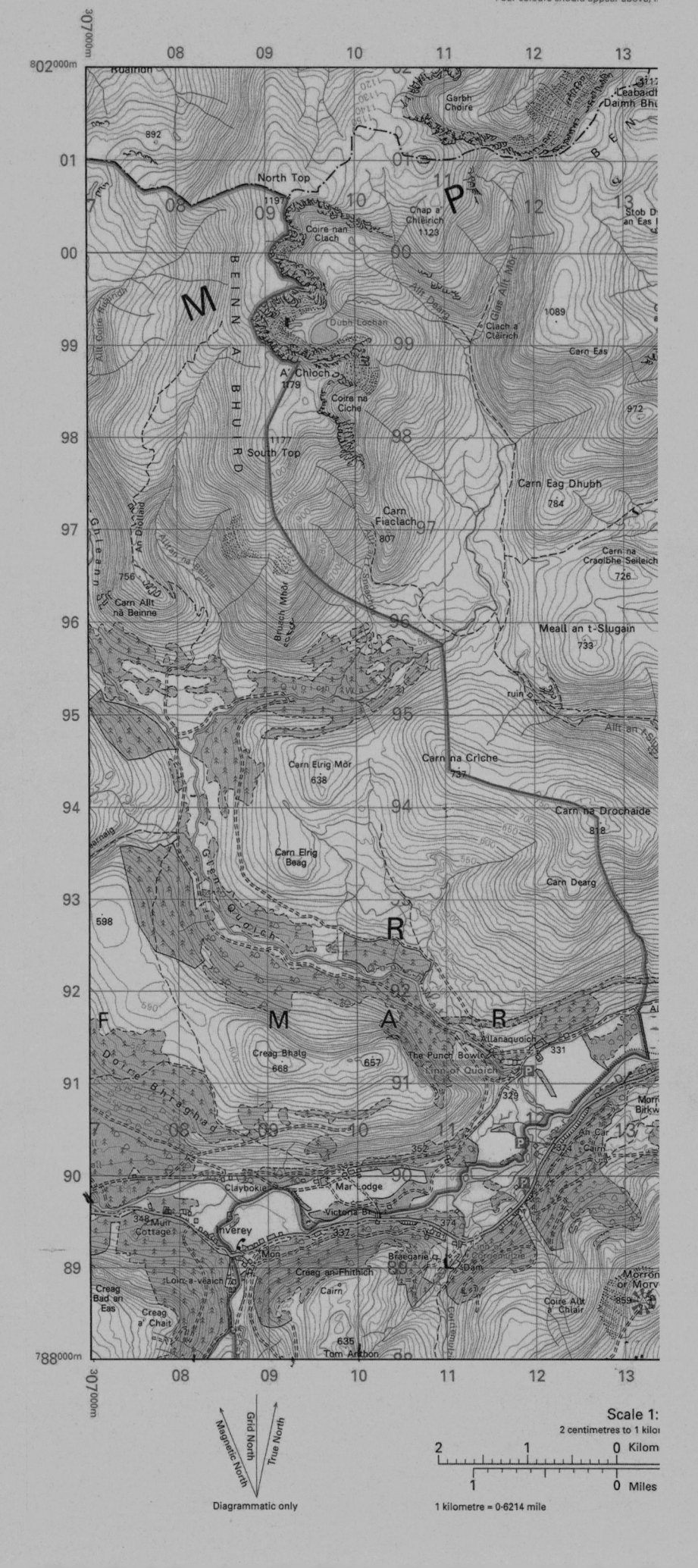

Extract No 1323/36/43

f not then please return to the invigilator.
f not then please return to the invigilator.

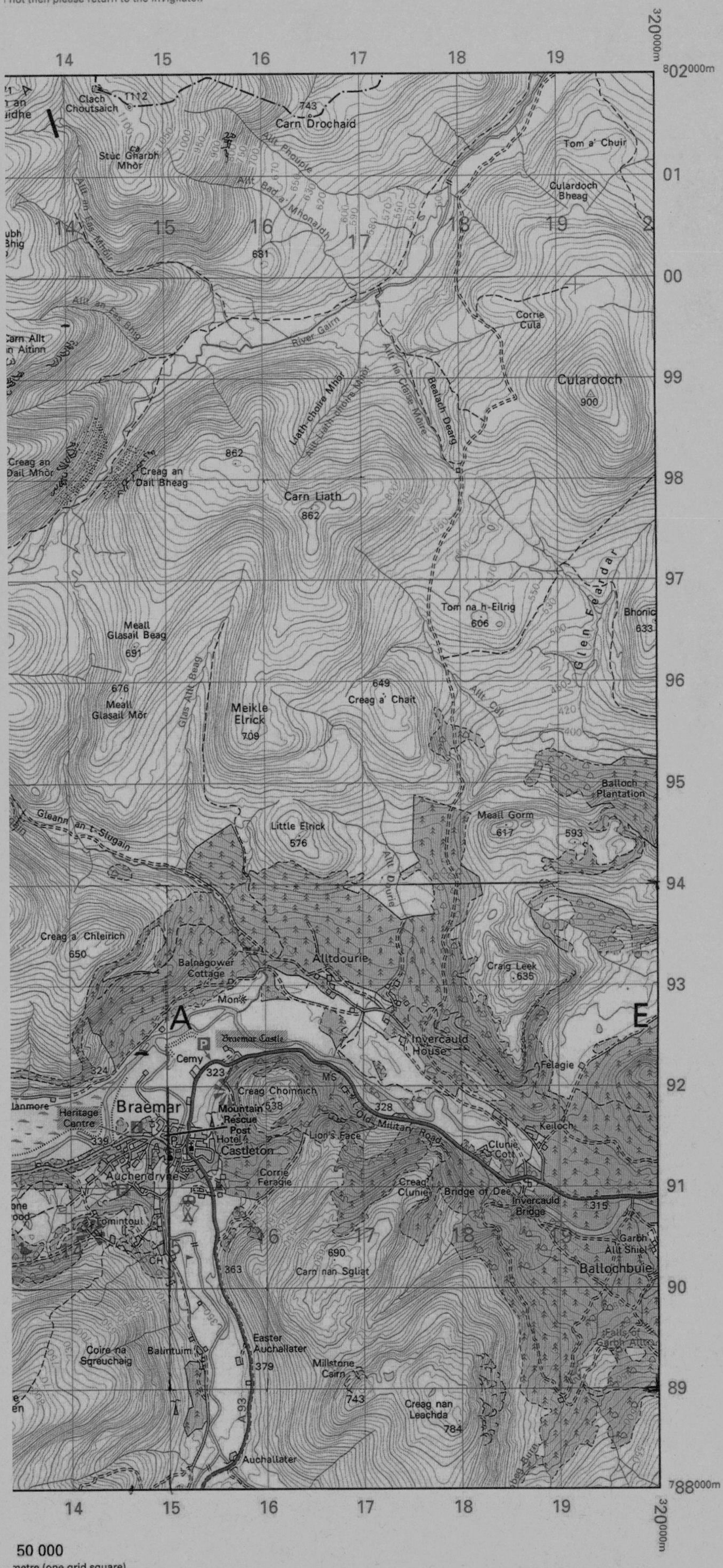

50 000
metre (one grid square)
etres 1 2 3
1 2

1 mile = 1·6093 kilometres

Practice Papers for SQA Exams: Higher Geography, Practice Exam 2, Paper 1

SECTION A

Answer all the questions in this section

Marks

QUESTION 1: Atmosphere

Study Diagram Q1A.

(a) **Describe** the characteristics of the tropical maritime and the tropical continental air masses. You should refer to the origin, nature and weather associated with each air mass.

8

Study Diagrams Q1B and Q1C.

(b) **Describe** and **explain** the variation in rainfall in West Africa.

10

Diagram Q1A: Selected air masses over Africa in January and July

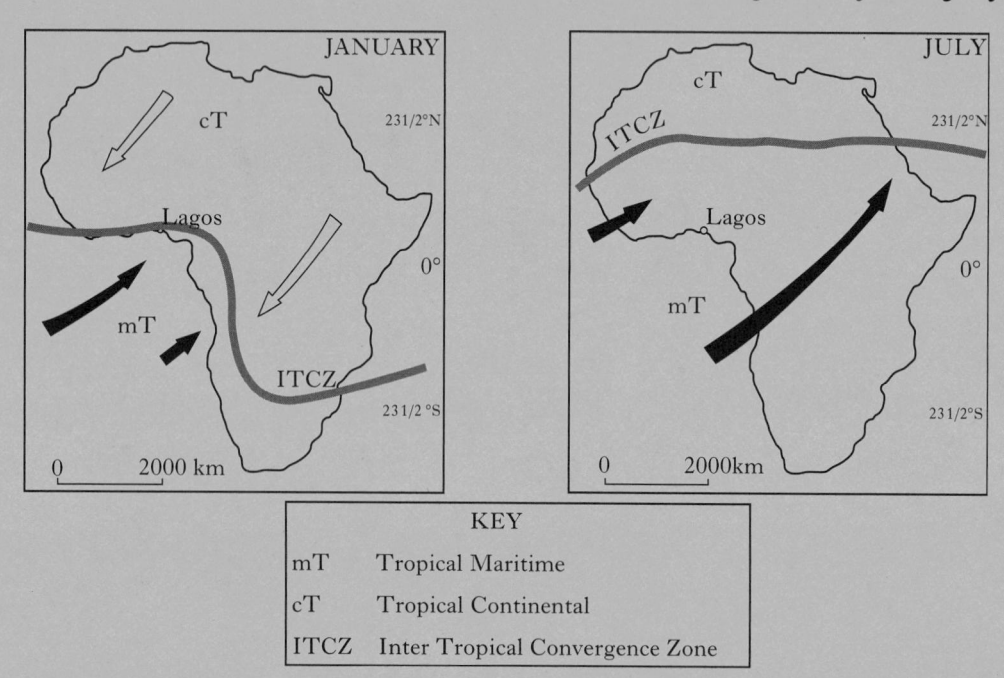

KEY
mT   Tropical Maritime
cT   Tropical Continental
ITCZ Inter Tropical Convergence Zone

Diagram Q1B: Precipitation data in millimetres for selected places in West Africa

	J	F	M	A	M	J	J	A	S	O	N	D
Lagos	36	41	132	163	290	452	294	53	154	200	66	28
Jos	3	4	19	98	182	200	302	296	222	46	4	1
Timbuktu	0	0	3	0	3	25	80	82	50	3	0	0

QUESTION 1: continued

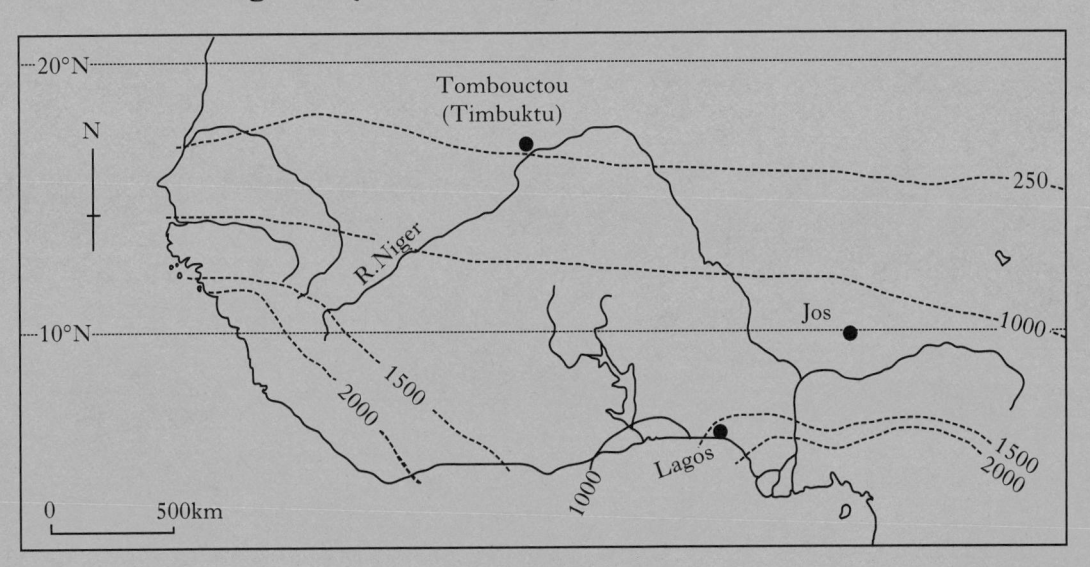

Marks

Diagram Q1C: Rainfall patterns in West Africa

50

KEY ------------ Isohyets showing mean annual rainfall (mm)

~~~ Rivers

QUESTION 2: Lithosphere

Study the map extract 1269/404 of Braemar.

(a) **Describe** the evidence which shows that the area covered by the map extract has been affected by glacial erosion. (You should refer to appropriate grid references and named features in your answer.)

8

(b) With the help of annotated diagrams, **explain** how **two** of the features you have named in part (a) were formed.

10

QUESTION 3: Rural Geography

(a) Study Diagram Q3A.

For an area that you have studied **describe** and **explain** the main characteristics of this farming system.

10

Diagram Q3A: Intensive peasant farming in the Ganges Valley, India

(b) This type of farming landscape has changed over the last twenty years. For an area you have studied, **explain** how these changes have affected the environment and the local people.

8

QUESTION 4: Industrial Geography

Study Diagram Q4.

(a) For a named industrial location in the European Union which you have studied, **explain** how such factors shown in Diagram Q4 originally attracted industry to the area.   **10**

(b) Many of the industries originally attracted to the area will have declined. **Describe** the factors which led to their decline and the impact of this on the environment.   **8**

Diagram Q4: Factors affecting the location of industry

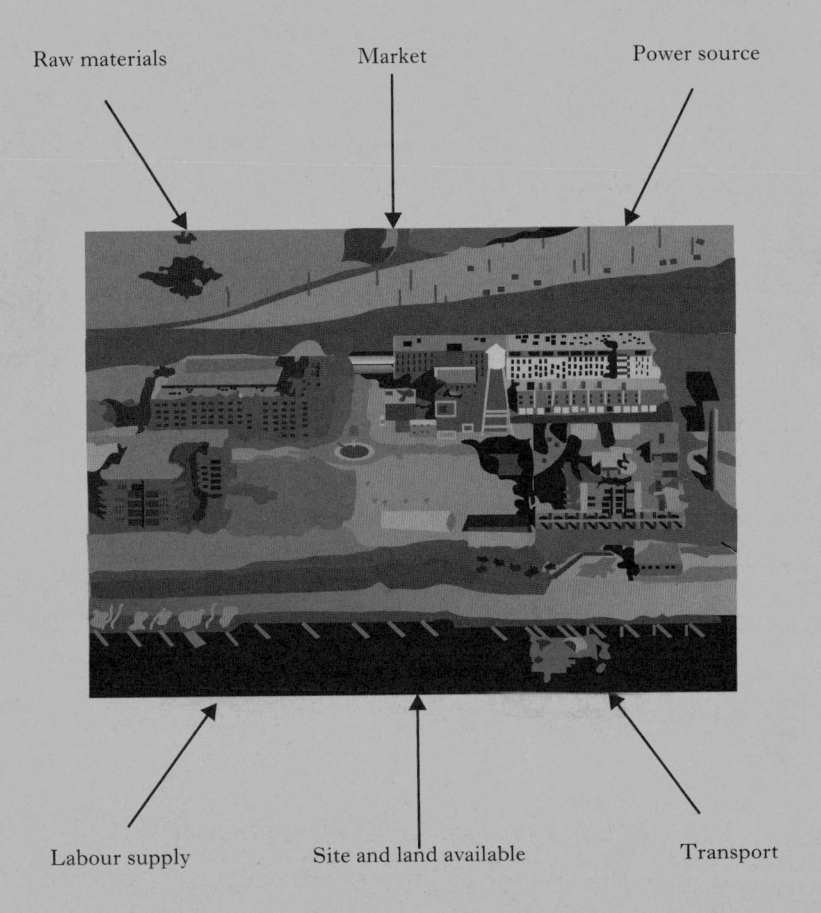

Raw materials   Market   Power source

Labour supply   Site and land available   Transport

SECTION B

**Answer ONE question from this section,
i.e. either Question 5 or Question 6**

Marks

QUESTION 5: Hydrosphere

(a) Using appropriate grid references, **describe** the physical characteristics of the River Dee **and** its valley between 100895 and 190907.

8

(b) Waterfalls are common features in the upper course of a river.

Explain with the aid of a diagram or diagrams how this feature is formed.

6

DO NOT ANSWER THIS QUESTION IF YOU HAVE ALREADY ANSWERED QUESTION 5

QUESTION 6: Biosphere

(a) **Describe** the main characteristics of the soil. (You should refer to the colour of the soil, the horizons, the texture and how well drained it is.)

6

Diagram Q6A: Three soil profiles

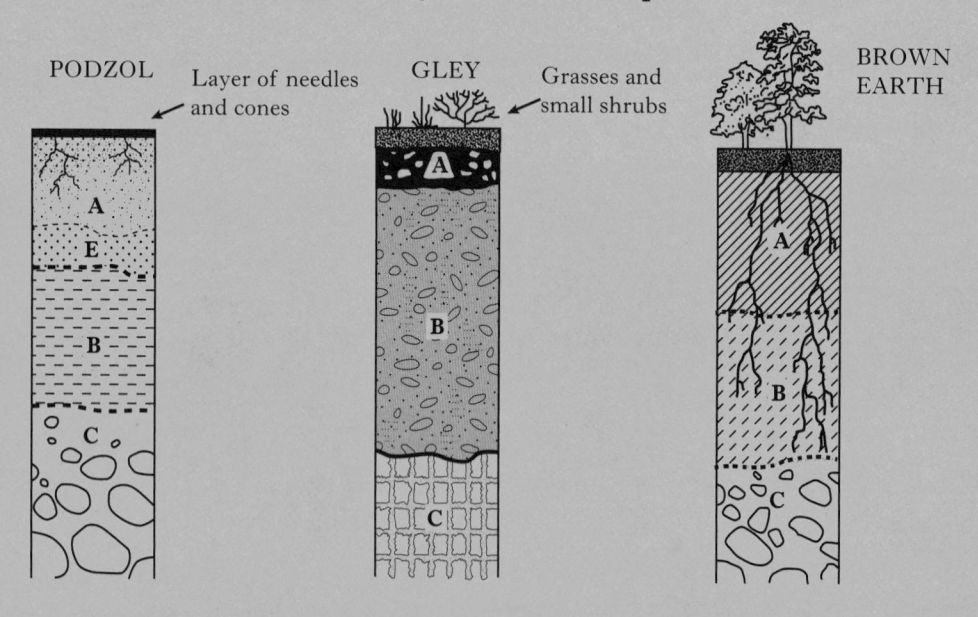

QUESTION 6: continued

Marks

(b) Diagram Q6B shows the main factors in soil formation.

Explain the physical factors which contributed to the formation of your chosen soil profile.

8

Diagram Q6B: Factors affecting soil formation

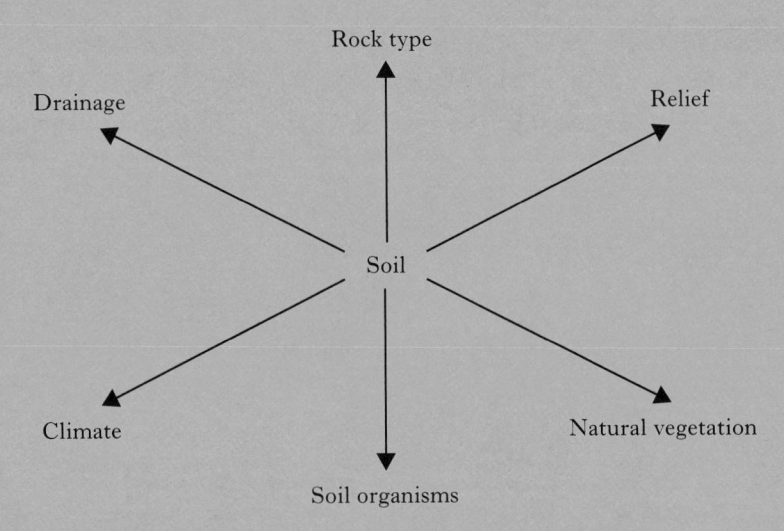

- Rock type
- Drainage
- Relief
- Climate
- Soil organisms
- Natural vegetation
- Soil (centre)

SECTION C

**Answer ONE question from this section,
i.e. either Question 7 or Question 8**

QUESTION 7: Population

Study Diagram Q7.

With reference to the migration of Turks to Germany, or any other population migration between two named countries you have studied:

(a) **Explain** the factors which encouraged people to move from Turkey to Germany or your chosen countries. (You should mention both push and pull factors in your answer.) **8**

(b) For your chosen countries in part (a), **comment** on the advantages and disadvantages which the migration has brought to either the country of origin or the receiving country. **6**

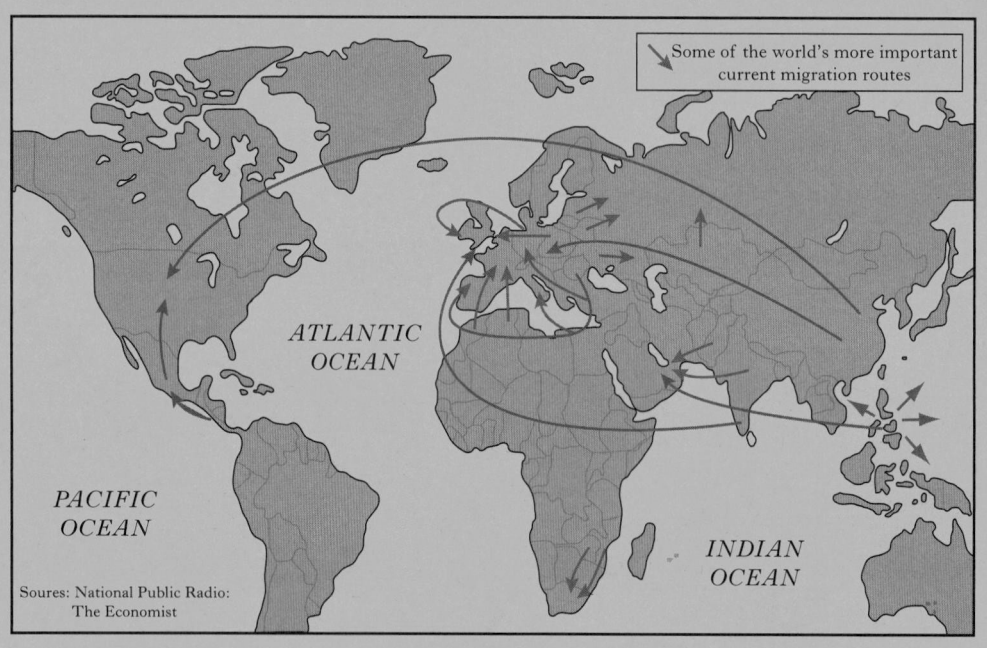

Diagram Q7: Recent international migration routes

DO NOT ANSWER THIS QUESTION IF YOU HAVE ALREADY ANSWERED QUESTION 7.

QUESTION 8: Urban Geography

(a) For Glasgow, or any named city in the developed world you have studied, **explain** how its site and situation led to its growth. **6**

(b) Study Diagram Q8 which shows part of Glasgow's city centre. Many city centres have undergone change over the last 20 years.

For Glasgow or a city you have studied, **describe** some of the changes that have taken place and suggest **reasons** for the changes. **8**

Diagram Q8: Part of Glasgow's city centre

[End of question paper]

Higher Geography

Practice Papers
For SQA Exams

Time allowed:
1 hour, 15 minutes

Exam 2, Paper 2

You should attempt **two** questions.

The marks available for each question are shown in the margin.

Marks will be given for suitable maps and diagrams, and for reference to named examples.

Write your answers in sentences.

Note   The reference maps and diagrams in this paper have been printed in black only: no other colours have been used.

QUESTION 1: Rural Land Resources

(a) Study Diagram Q1A.

For any named National Park you have studied, **explain** the social and economic opportunities provided by the landscape. **10**

(b) The Yorkshire Dales is an area of carboniferous limestone in the UK.

For this area or any other area of carboniferous limestone you have studied, **describe** the main physical features of the landscape, and **explain** with the use of annotated diagrams how these features were formed. (Your answer should refer to both surface **and** underground features.) **20**

(c) Study Diagram Q1B.

Some areas of the Yorkshire Dales have become 'honeypot sites'.

For the Yorkshire Dales, or any other popular area in a National Park you have studied,

(i) **Explain** why the area is popular with visitors. **6**

(ii) **Describe** the benefits these visitors bring to the people who live and work in the area. **6**

(iii) Large numbers of visitors can also bring problems to the area. **Describe two** of these problems and suggest ways of reducing the problems. **8**

(50)

Diagram Q1A: National Parks in Great Britain

Practice Papers for SQA Exams: Higher Geography, Practice Exam 2, Paper 2

Marks

QUESTION 1: continued

Diagram Q1B: Malham Cove in the Yorkshire Dales

QUESTION 2: Rural Land Degradation

(a) Look at Diagram Q2A.

Describe the rainfall patterns shown on the graph and explain why changing rainfall patterns may lead to land degradation.   **12**

(b) Look at Diagram Q2B.

Choose three of the factors listed and, referring to areas you have studied in either Africa, north of the equator or the Amazon Basin,

(i) **explain** how each factor can lead to degradation;   **14**

(ii) **describe** the impact of land degradation on the people and the environment.   **16**

(c) Look at Diagram Q2C.

Choose any two methods of soil conservation shown on the diagram. Explain how each helps to conserve and reduce soil erosion.   **8**

(50)

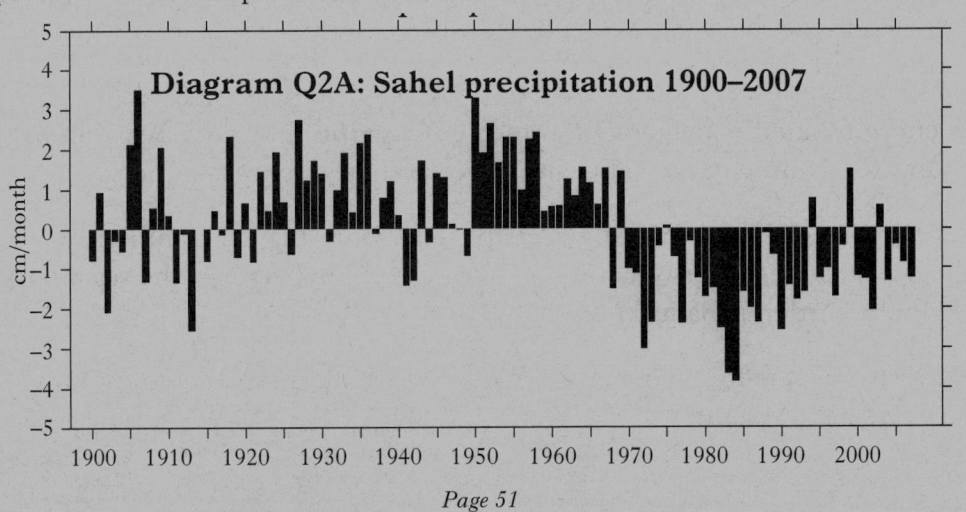

Diagram Q2A: Sahel precipitation 1900–2007

QUESTION 2: continued

Diagram Q2B: Some causes of land degradation

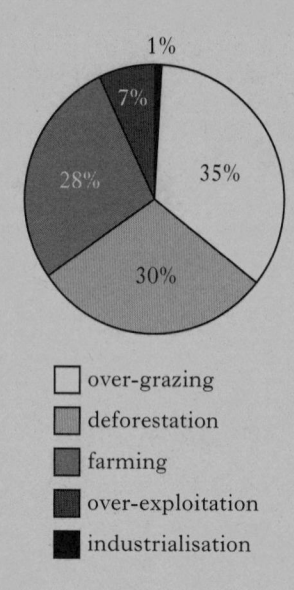

- over-grazing 35%
- deforestation 30%
- farming 28%
- over-exploitation 7%
- industrialisation 1%

Diagram Q2C: Some soil conservation methods

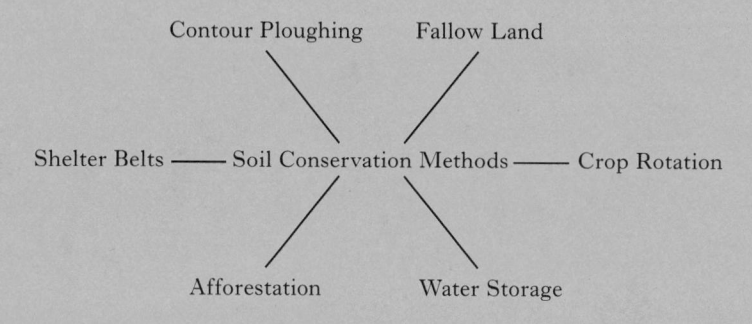

Contour Ploughing, Fallow Land, Shelter Belts, Crop Rotation, Afforestation, Water Storage — Soil Conservation Methods

QUESTION 3: River Basin Management

(a) Look at Diagrams Q3A and Q3B.

Explain how river basin management projects can affect the hydrological cycle of a river basin. **10**

(b) Look at Diagram Q3C.

'The Colorado River is one of the most dammed and controlled rivers in the world.'

With reference to the Colorado River Scheme or any other water management project you have studied in North America, Asia or Africa, explain the the physical and human factors that have to be considered when choosing sites for dams and their associated reservoirs. **10**

(c) For your chosen water management project, **describe** and **explain** the social, economic and environmental benefits and adverse consequences of the project. **24**

(d) 'The Colorado brings life to 21 million people and more than two million acres of farmland in seven states and two countries. The river finally enters the sea 50 miles south of the US border at Baja, Mexico.'

Describe problems that might occur when rivers such as the Colorado run through more than one state or country. **6**

(50)

QUESTION 3: continued

Diagram Q3A: Hydrological cycle

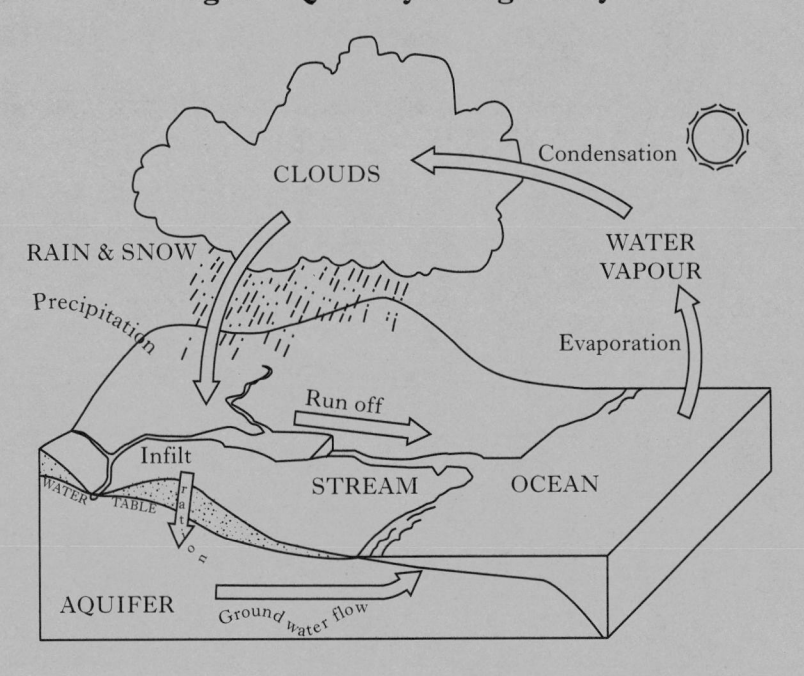

Diagram Q3B: Some aims of multi-purpose River Basin Management

- Improve water supply
- Control flooding
- Production of HEP
- Better navigation

Diagram Q3C: Selected Colorado River dams

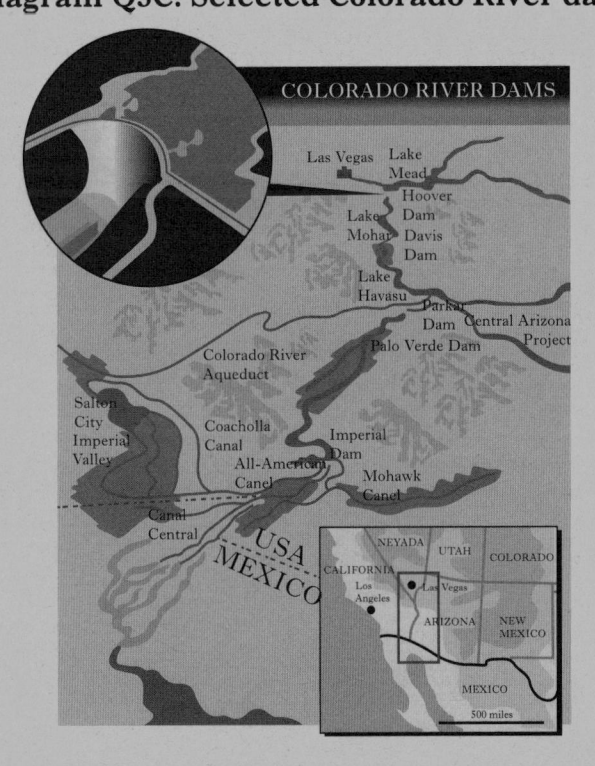

QUESTION 4: Urban Change and its Management

Marks

(a) Look at Map Q4A.

'The world's largest cities will increasingly be located in less-developed countries.'

Suggest reasons why most cities forecast to have over 10 million people in 2015 are located in the poorer countries of the world. Refer to cities you have studied in your answer. **12**

(b) Look at Diagram Q4B.

For Mumbai, or any other named city you have studied in a developing country:

(i) **describe** difficulties which have resulted from its rapid growth (you should refer to social, economic and environmental difficulties in your answer);

(ii) **describe** some methods which can be used to solve these problems; and

(iii) **describe** how successful have these methods been. **20**

(c) Study Diagram Q4C.

The diagram shows selected problems which have occurred in developed world cities over the last 50 years. Choose one of the problems shown and with reference to a named city you have studied in the developed world:

(i) **suggest** some causes of the problem;

(ii) **describe** methods used to solve the problem;

(iii) **describe** how successful have these methods been. **18**

(50)

Map Q4A: Cities with more than 10 million people in 2015

19. Istanbul, Turkey
21. Moscow, Russian Federation
20. Beijing, China
11. Karachi, Pakistan
15. Shanghai, China
14. Los Angeles, **U.S.A
6. New York, *U.S.A.
10. Calcutta, India
1. Tokyo, Japan
22. Paris, France
18. Osaka-Kobe, Japan
13. Cairo, Egypt
7. Dhaka, Bangladesh
4. Mexico City, Mexico
16. Manila, Philippines
9. Lagos, Nigeria
3. Delhi, India
17. Rio de Janeiro, Brazil
2. Mumbai, India
8. Jakarta, Indonesia
5. São Paulo, Brazil
12. Buenos Aires, Argentina

- 10-15 million people
- 16-19 million people
- 20-37 million people

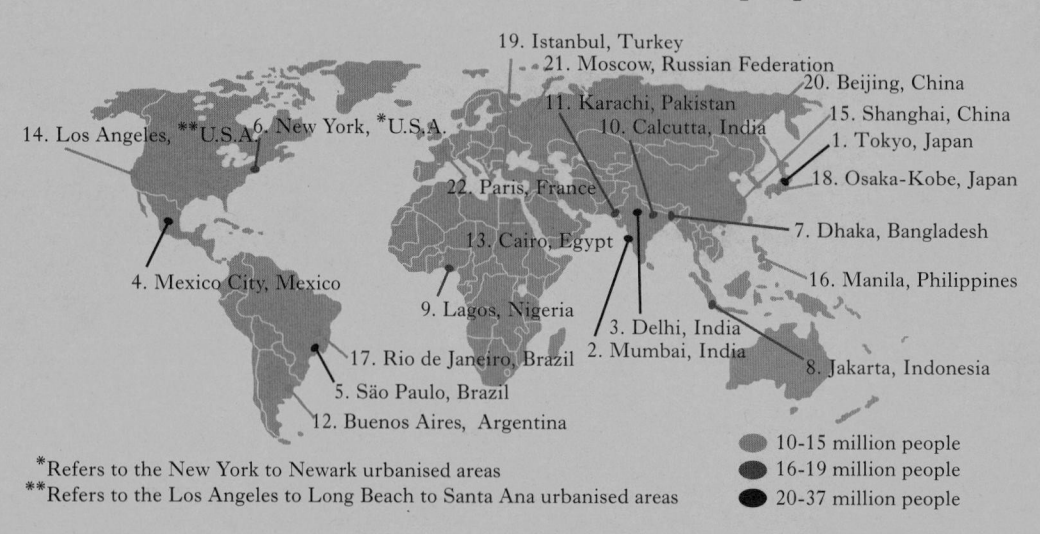

*Refers to the New York to Newark urbanised areas
**Refers to the Los Angeles to Long Beach to Santa Ana urbanised areas

QUESTION 4: continued

Diagram Q4B: Population growth, Mumbai

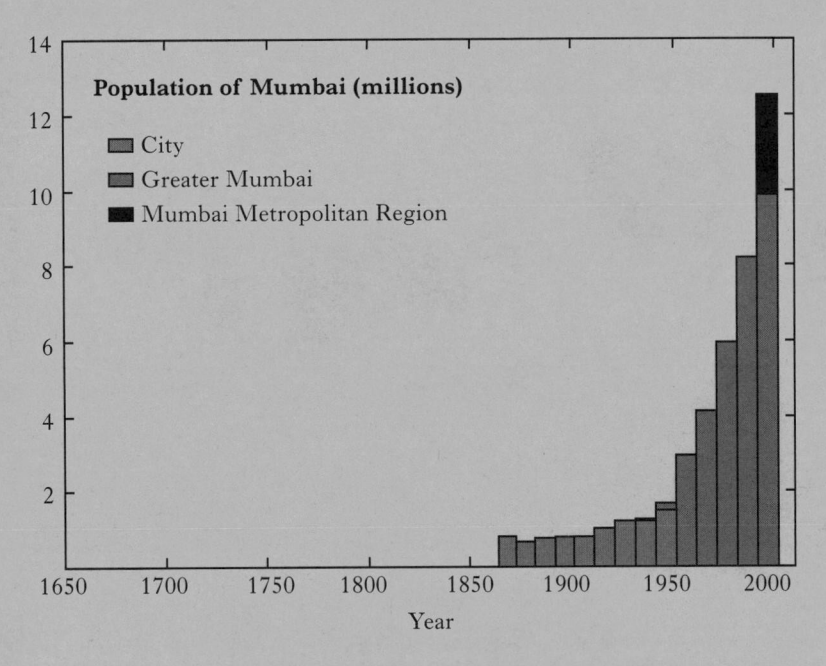

Population of Mumbai (millions)
- City
- Greater Mumbai
- Mumbai Metropolitan Region

Diagram Q4C: Selected problems of developed world cities

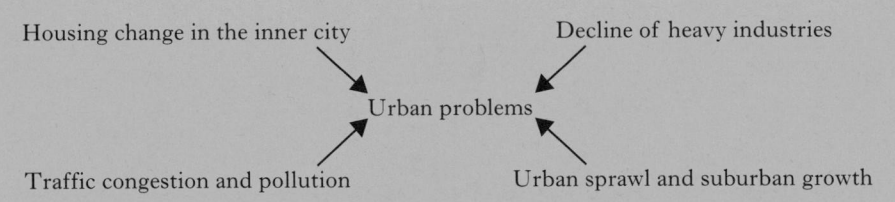

Housing change in the inner city → Urban problems ← Decline of heavy industries
Traffic congestion and pollution → Urban problems ← Urban sprawl and suburban growth

QUESTION 5: Development and Health

(a) Identify **one** social and **one** economic indicator.

For each **explain** how it might show how developed a country is. **6**

(b) **Explain** why variations in development can exist **between** developing countries.

You should refer to named countries you have studied in your answer. **10**

(c) Levels of development can vary greatly in different areas in a **developing** country.

For a named country you have studied, **suggest reasons** for the variations in development. **10**

(d) Diagram Q5 shows areas of the world with malaria outbreaks.

For **either** cholera, **or** bilharzia, or malaria:

(i) **describe** the human and environmental conditions which put people at risk of catching your chosen disease;

(ii) **describe** measures which can be used to try and control the disease, and

(iii) for the measures you have described in part (ii) comment on how successful they have been. **24**

(50)

QUESTION 5: continued

Marks

Diagram Q5: Malaria endemic areas

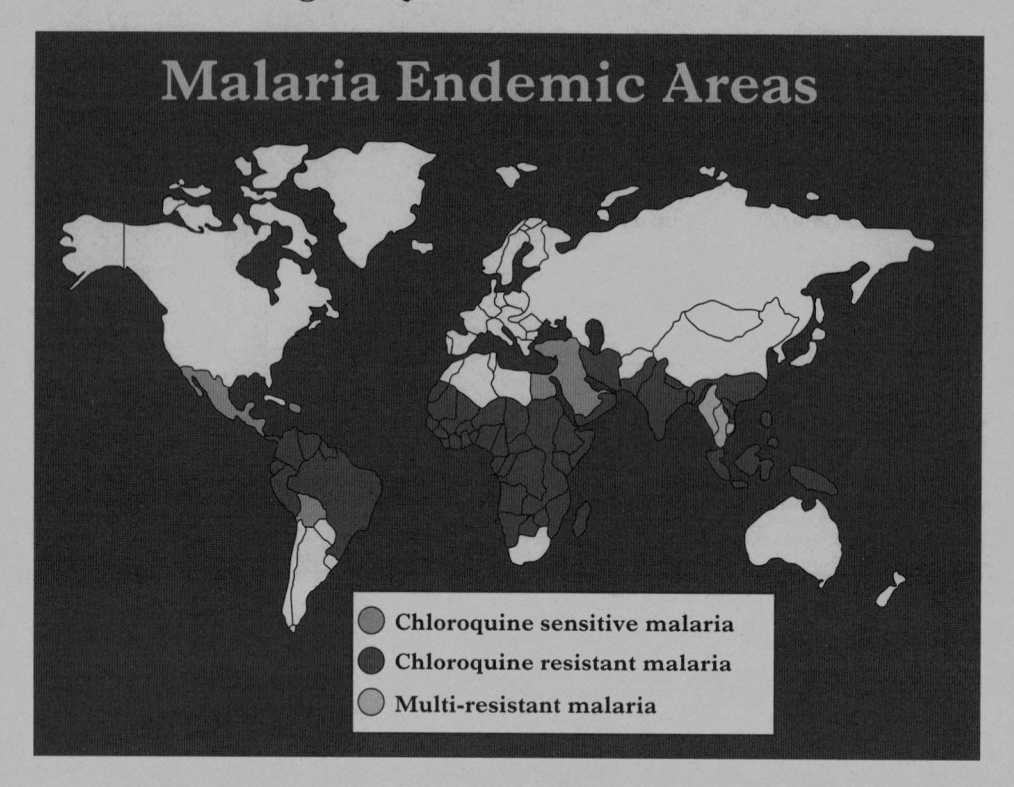

Malaria Endemic Areas

- Chloroquine sensitive malaria
- Chloroquine resistant malaria
- Multi-resistant malaria

[End of question paper]

Higher Geography

| Practice Papers | Time allowed: | **Exam 3, Paper 1** |
| For SQA Exams | 1 hour, 30 minutes | |

You should attempt **six** questions:

- **every** question in **Section A** (Questions 1, 2, 3 and 4);
- **one** question in **Section B** (Question 5 **or** Question 6);
- **one** question in **Section C** (Question 7 **or** Question 8).

The marks available for each question are shown in the margin.

Marks will be given for suitable maps and diagrams, and for reference to named examples.

Write your answers in sentences.

Note   The reference maps and diagrams in this paper have been printed in black only: no other colours have been used.

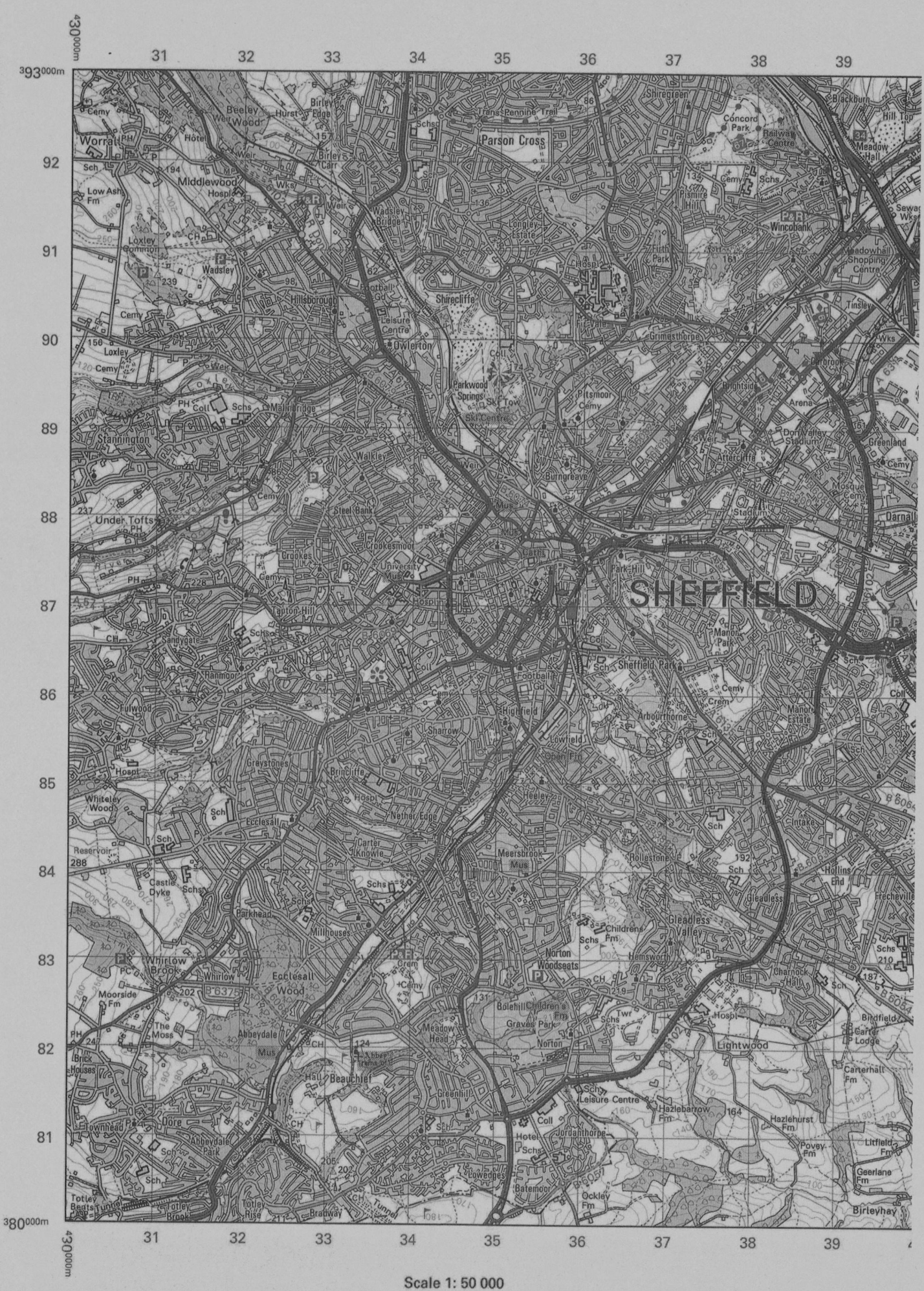

Scale 1: 50 000
2 centimetres to 1 kilometre (one grid square)

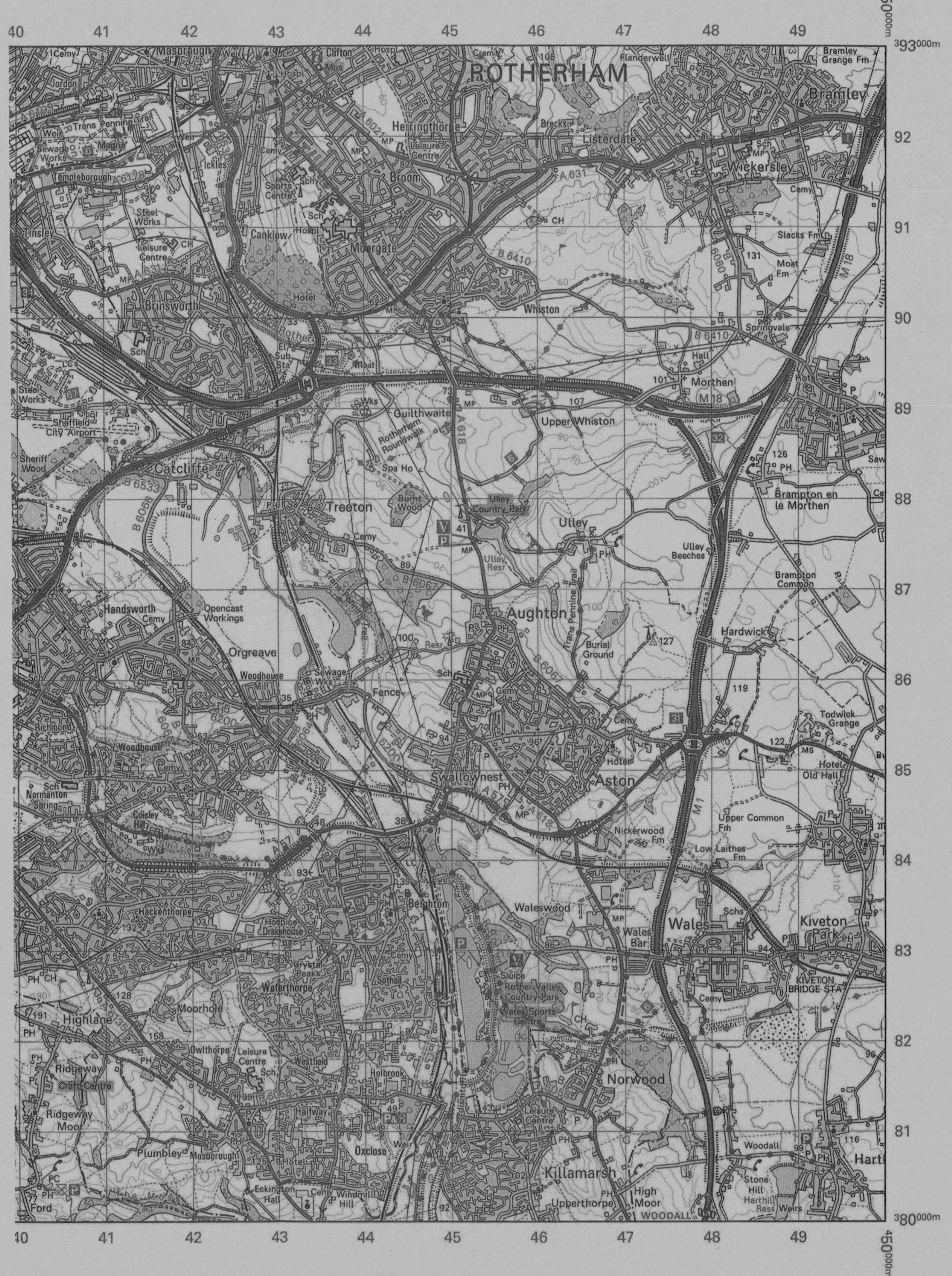

ROTHERHAM
Masbrough
Clifton
Herringthorpe
Broom
Moorgate
Canklow
Brinsworth
Whiston
Upper Whiston
Wickersley
Bramley
Listerdale
Flanderwell
Morthen
Brampton en le Morthen
Guilthwaite
Treeton
Catcliffe
Ulley
Ulley Country Park
Aughton
Handsworth
Orgreave
Woodhouse Mill
Fence
Swallownest
Aston
Woodhouse
Richmond
Normanton Spring
Coisley Hill
Hackenthorpe
Beighton
Drakehouse
Crystal Peaks
Waterthorpe
Sothall
Rother Valley Country Park
Waleswood
Wales
Wales Bar
Kiveton Park
Hardwick
Todwick Grange
Highlane
Ridgeway
Ridgeway Moor
Moorhole
Owlthorpe
Westfield
Holbrook
Halfway
Oxclose
Plumbley
Mosborough
Eckington Hall
Killamarsh
Norwood
Upperthorpe
High Moor
Woodall
Stone Hill
Sheffield City Airport
Templeborough
Tinsley
Trans Pennine Trail
M1
M18
A631
A618
A57
B6410
B6067
B6533
B6200
B6058
393000m
380000m
450000m
40
41
42
43
44
45
46
47
48
49

SECTION A

Answer all the questions in this section

Marks

QUESTION 1: Lithosphere

Study Diagram Q1A, which shows a coastal area in the UK.

(a) **Explain**, with the aid of a diagram or diagrams, how feature X shown in Diagram Q1A was formed.

10

Diagram Q1A: Coastal area in Pembrokeshire

(b) Look at Diagram Q1B.

Describe the conditions and processes involved which have led to the cliff collapsing.

8

Diagram Q1B: Cliff collapse

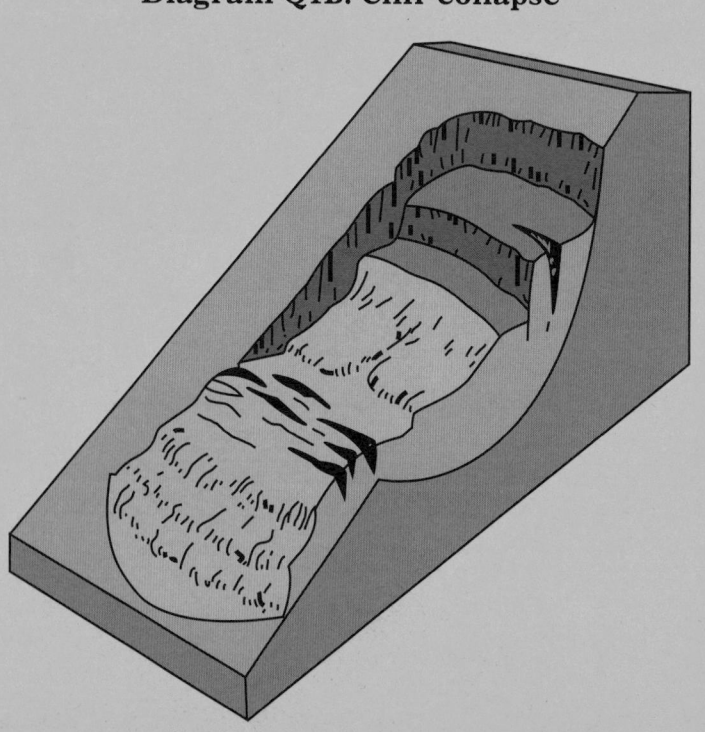

Practice Papers for SQA Exams: Higher Geography, Practice Exam 3, Paper 1

Marks

QUESTION 2: Biosphere

(a) Study Diagram Q2.

Describe and give reasons for the changes in plant types likely to be found as you move inland, away from the coast, across the transect shown in Diagram Q2 below. You should refer to specific plant types in your answer.   **12**

(b) **Explain** what is meant by the term 'climax vegetation'.   **6**

Diagram Q2: A transect across a sand dune coastline

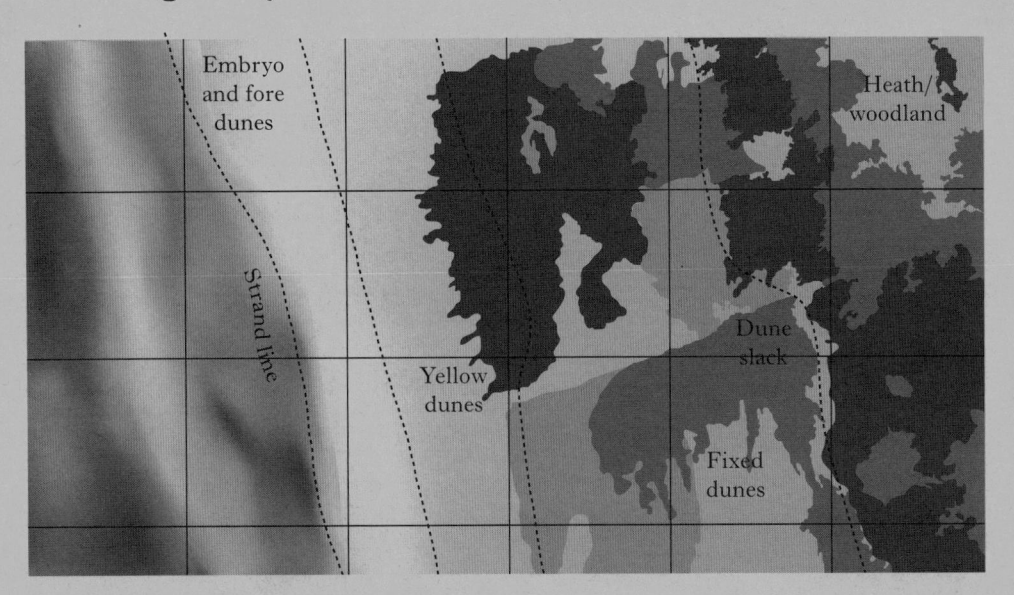

QUESTION 3: Population

Look at Diagram Q3.

(a) **Describe** the ways in which developed countries, such as the UK, can collect accurate population data.   **6**

(b) (i) Give reasons to **explain** why developing countries find it difficult to collect population data.

(ii) Why might the data collected not be as reliable as the data collected by a developed country?   **12**

Diagram Q3: National Statistics

The collection of accurate population data provides vital information on the population. It helps to develop public services and shape the future of a country.

Practice Papers for SQA Exams: Higher Geography, Practice Exam 3, Paper 1

QUESTION 4: Industrial Geography

Marks

Look at Diagram Q4A.

(a) For Central Scotland, or any other industrial concentration in the European Union which you have studied, **describe** the factors which led to the growth of traditional industries before 1950.

8

Diagram Q4A: Clydebridge Steel Works

Look at Diagram Q4B.

(b) For Central Scotland, or any other industrial concentration in the EU, **explain** the human and economic factors that influence the location of new industrial developments.

10

Diagram Q4B: Eurocentral Industrial Park

SECTION B

**Answer ONE question from this section,
i.e. either Question 5 or Question 6**

QUESTION 5: Atmosphere

(*a*) **Explain** the ways in which the circulation cells in the atmosphere help to redistribute energy between areas of surplus and deficit. **8**

(*b*) Study Diagram Q5.

Describe and **explain** the world pattern of ocean currents shown in Diagram Q5. **6**

Diagram Q5: Ocean currents

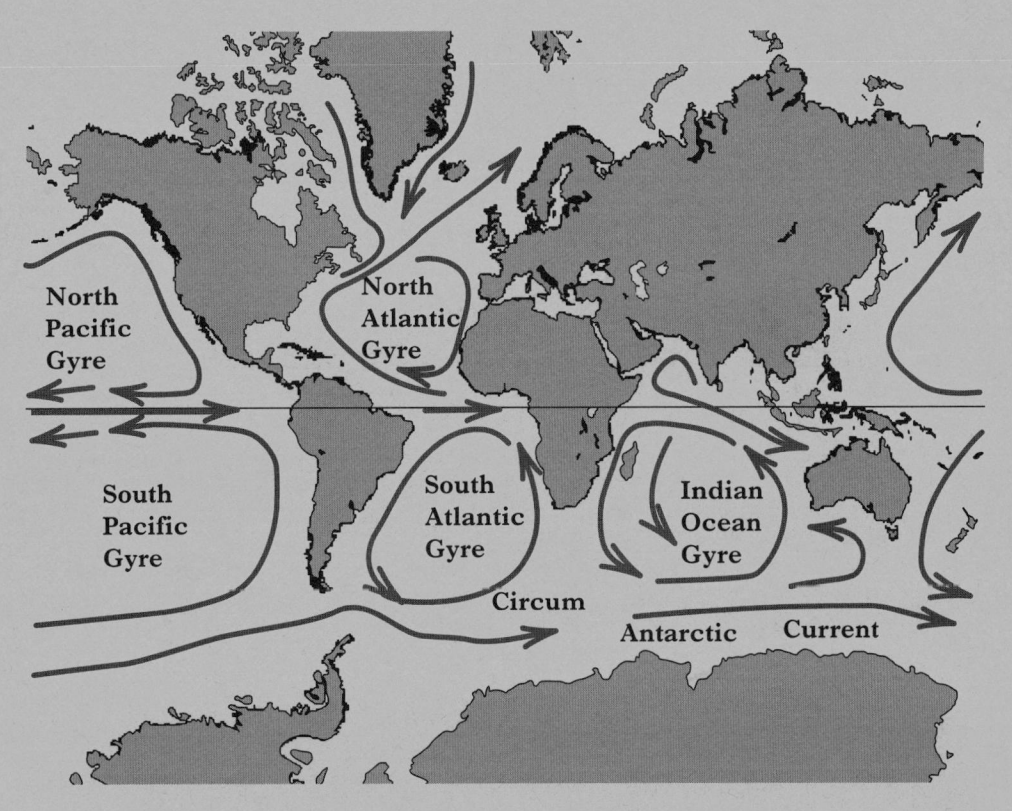

**DO NOT ANSWER THIS QUESTION IF YOU HAVE
ALREADY ANSWERED QUESTION 5**

QUESTION 6: Hydrosphere

Study Diagrams 6A and 6B.

(a) **Describe** the processes involved in the continuous movement of water around the earth and its atmosphere (hydrological cycle) **6**

(b) There are differences between hydrographs in rural and urban areas.

Give reasons to **explain** these differences. **8**

Diagram Q6A: Hydrograph for a wooded, rural area

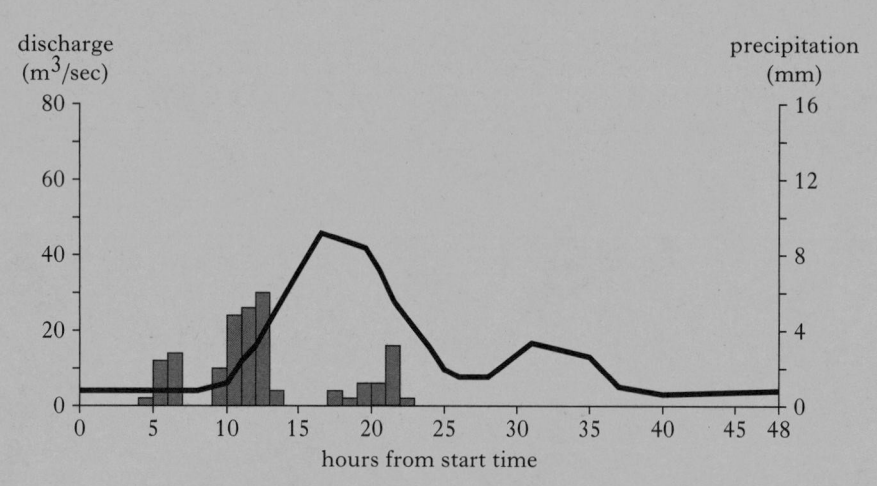

Diagram Q6B: Hydrograph for an urban area

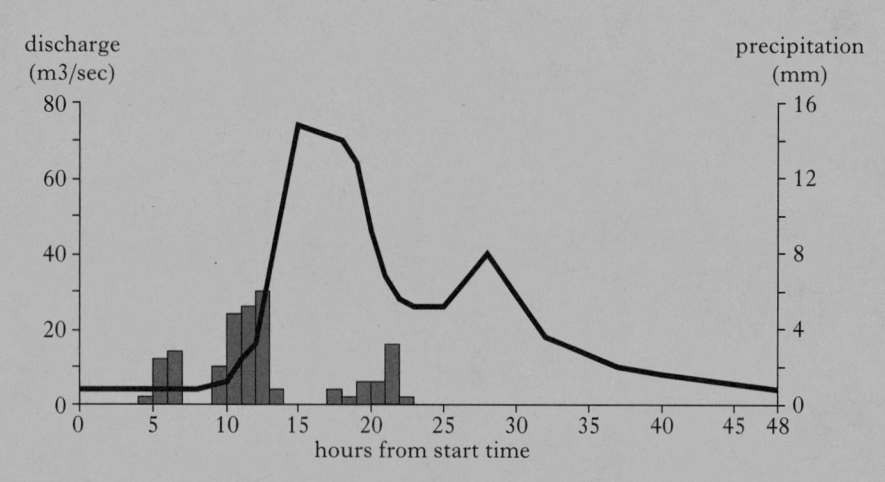

SECTION C

**Answer ONE question from this section,
i.e. either Question 7 or Question 8**

QUESTION 7: Rural Geography

Study Diagrams Q7A, Q7B and Q7C.

(a) Select **one** of the farming systems in the diagrams below.

   Describe and explain the main characteristics of your chosen farming type. (You should refer to a named location in your answer.)   **6**

(b) Many farming systems have been subjected to change.

For **one** of the farming systems shown in Diagrams Q7A, Q7B and Q7C below, **describe** how changes in the farming systems have affected the environment and the people.   **8**

Diagram Q7A: Shifting cultivation

Diagram Q7B: Intensive peasant farming

Diagram Q7C: Extensive commercial farming

DO NOT ANSWER THIS QUESTION IF YOU HAVE ALREADY ANSWERED QUESTION 7

QUESTION 8: Urban Geography

Study OS Map Extract number 1491/111: Sheffield and Diagram Q8A.

(a) Area A (grid square 3487) and Area B (grid square 3480) are two residential areas in Sheffield.

   Describe the residential environments of both areas, and **suggest reasons** for their differences. **8**

Diagram Q8A: Sheffield

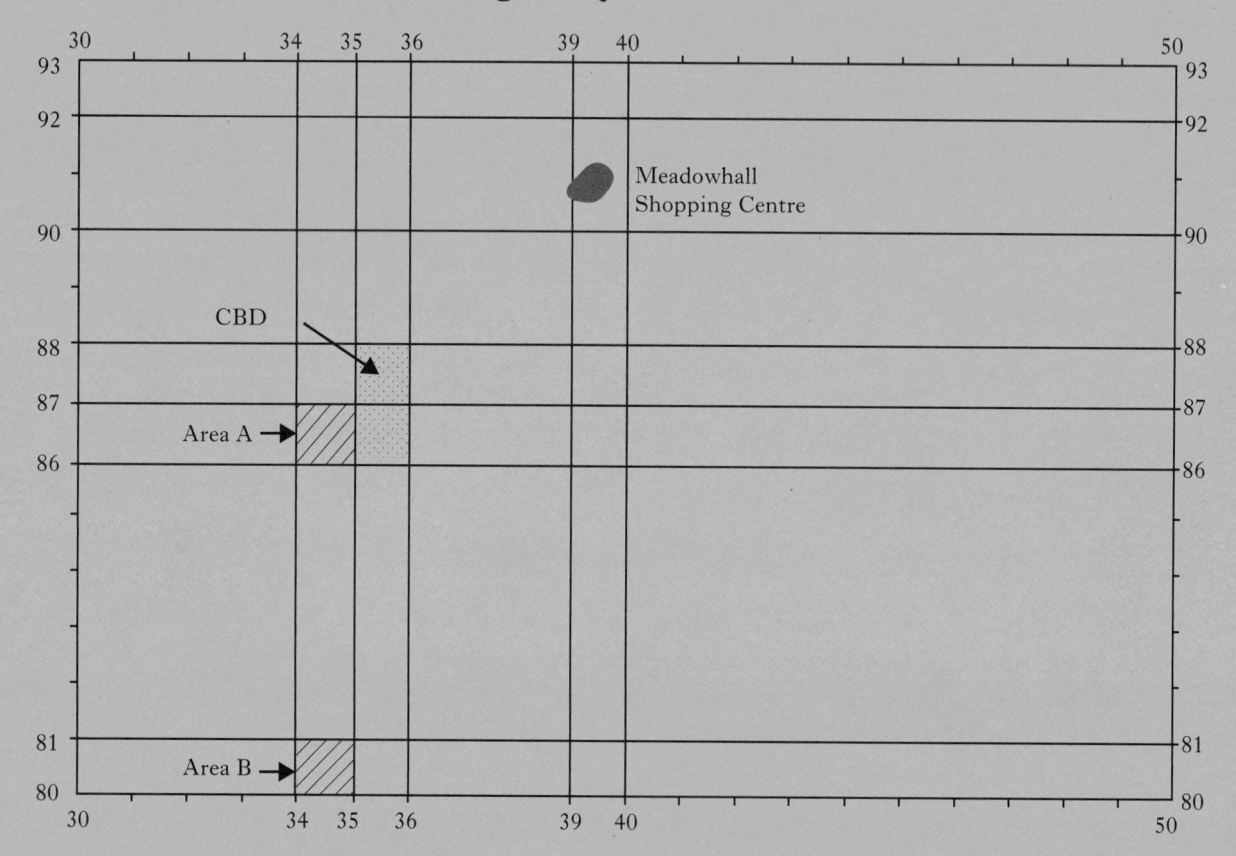

(b) Study Diagrams Q8A, Q8B, Q8C and the map extract.

   Meadowhall Shopping Centre (GR 3990 and 3991) opened in 1990 on the site of a former steel works.

   Using map evidence, and Diagrams Q8A, Q8B and Q8C, **explain** why this is a good site for the indoor shopping centre. **6**

QUESTION 8: continued

Diagram Q8B: Aerial view of Meadowhall Shopping Centre

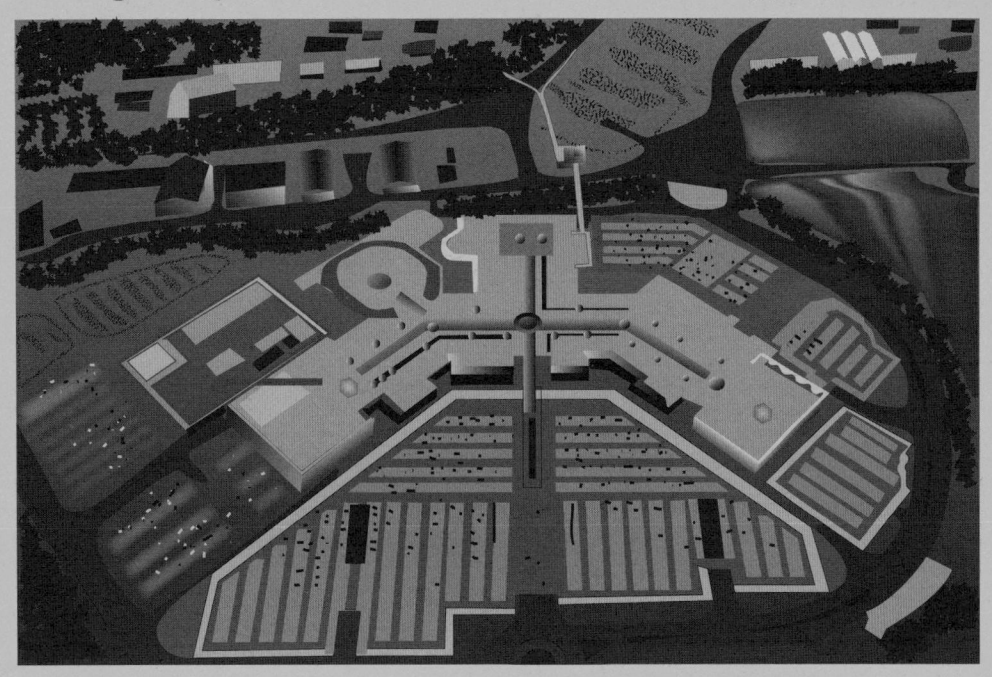

Diagram Q8C: Location of Meadowhall Shopping Centre

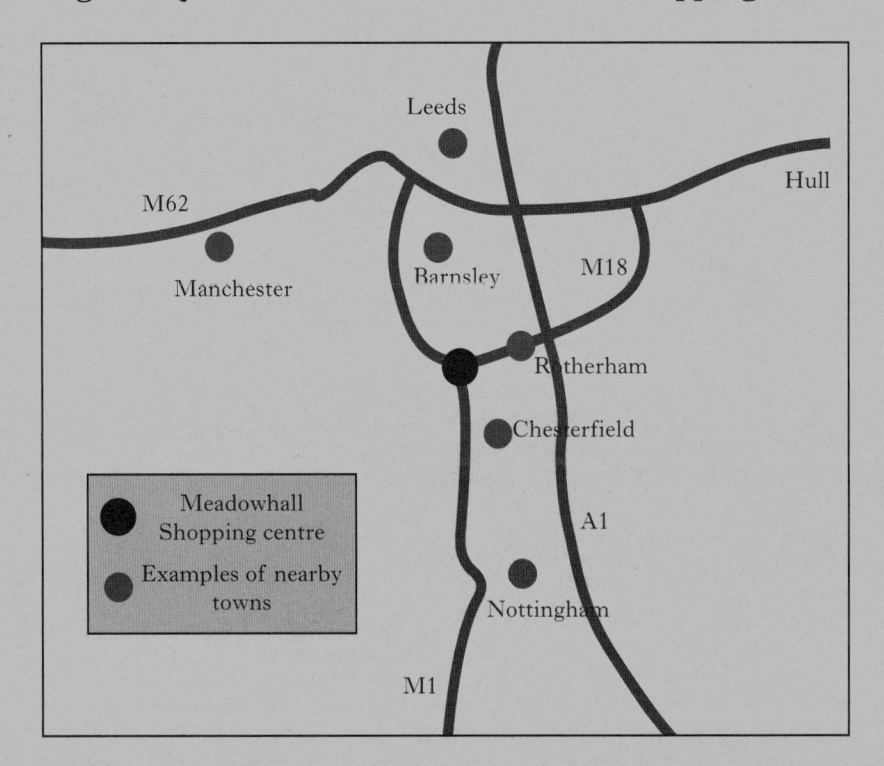

[End of question paper]

Higher Geography

Practice Papers Time allowed: Exam 3, Paper 2
For SQA Exams 1 hour, 15 minutes

You should attempt **two** questions.

The marks available for each question are shown in the margin.

Marks will be given for suitable maps and diagrams, and for reference to named examples.

Write your answers in sentences.

Note   The reference maps and diagrams in this paper have been printed in black only: no other colours have been used.

QUESTION 1: Rural Land Resources

'The Lake District is one of Britain's popular National Parks. Areas like Windermere and Helvellyn are at risk because of the high number of visitors throughout the year.'

Conservation spokesperson

Study Diagram Q1 and the quote above.

(a) For the Lake District or any other National Park you have studied, **explain** why it is popular with tourists. **10**

(b) The Lake District is famous for its glaciated scenery. For the Lake District or any other National Park with glaciated scenery:

   (i) **describe** some of the environmental problems which have arisen in your chosen park.

   (ii) **outline** ways that the problems mentioned in part (i) can be tackled, and comment on how successful they have been. **20**

(c) **Describe**, with the aid of annotated diagrams, the main physical features found in the Lake District or any other area of glaciated scenery that you have studied, and **explain** how they were formed. **20**

(50)

Diagram Q1: Lake District National Park

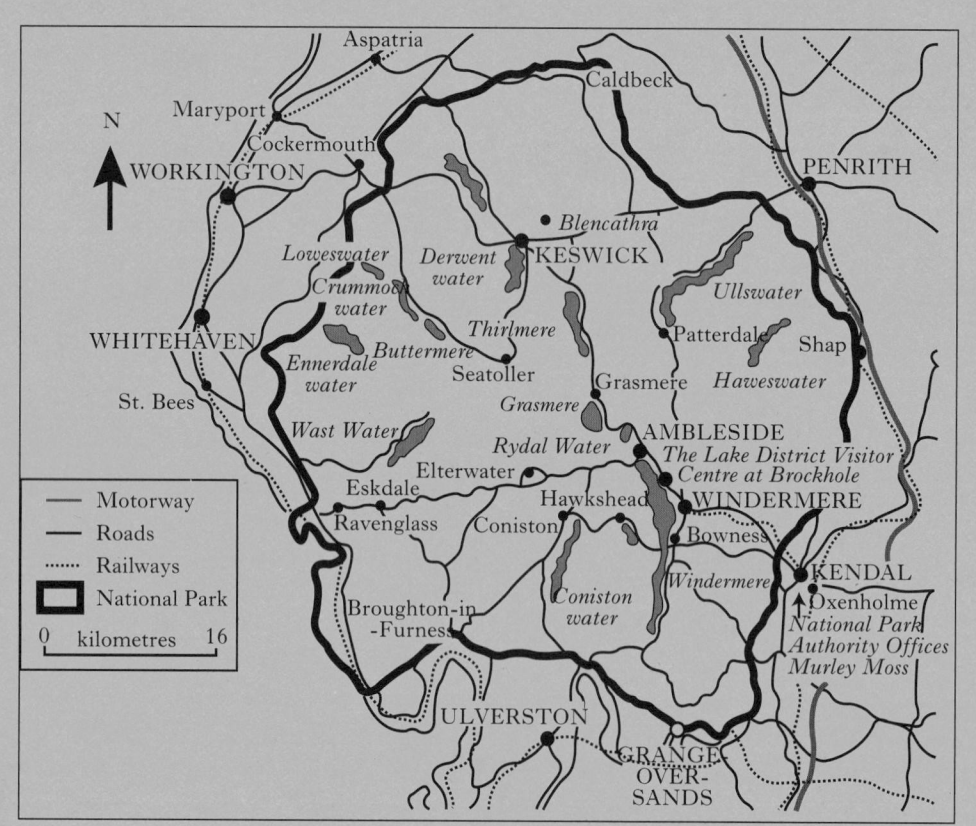

QUESTION 2: Rural Land Degradation

Marks

(a) **Describe** and **explain** the processes involved in wind erosion. **6**

(b) For either Africa, north of the Equator, or the Amazon Basin, explain how physical and human factors contribute to land degradation. **18**

(c) Look at Diagram Q2A.

For an area you have studied in Africa, north of the Equator, or North America:

(i) **describe** methods that can be used to help prevent soil erosion;

(ii) **explain** how your chosen methods help to conserve soil in rural areas. **18**

(d) Look at Diagram Q2B.

Explain how inappropriate farming activities contributed to the creation of the Dust Bowl of North America. **8**

(50)

Diagram Q2A: Physical impacts of desertification

- Soil erosion
- Sun-baked, cracked soil
- Loss of plants and animals
- Gullying
- Dry rivers
- Growth of deserts
- Increase in sand storms
- Flash floods

Diagram Q2B: Farming practices in the Dust Bowl, North America

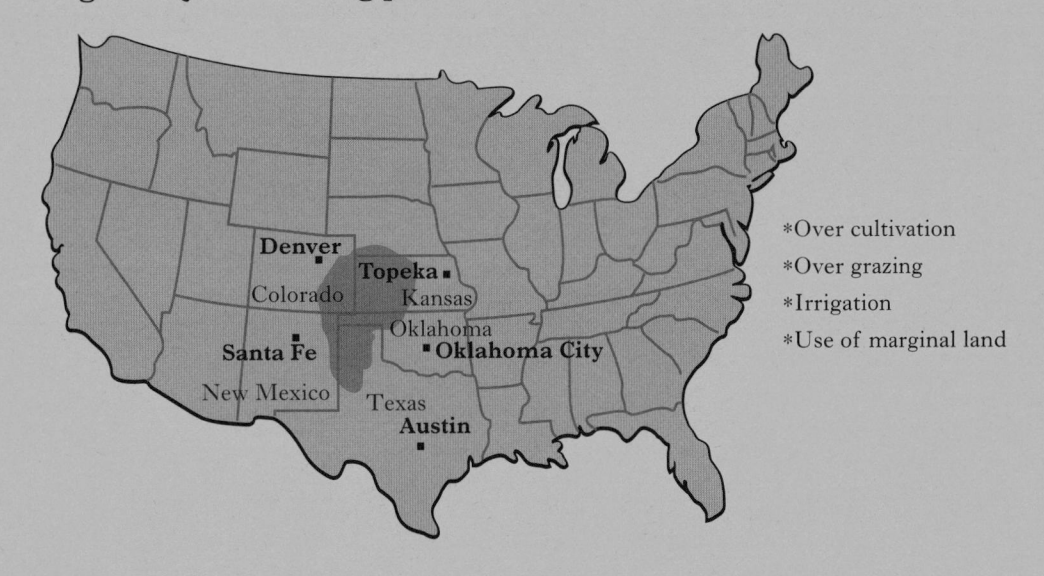

*Over cultivation
*Over grazing
*Irrigation
*Use of marginal land

QUESTION 3: River Basin Management

Marks

(a) Study Map Q3A.

 Describe and **explain** the general distribution of the main river basins in Africa. **10**

(b) Study Map Q3B and Map Q3C.

 Explain why there is a need for water management in Egypt. **10**

(c) For the Nile or any other named water control project you have studied in Africa, Asia or North America, **describe** and **explain** the social, economic and environmental benefits and adverse effects of the scheme. **24**

(d) 'The main conflicts in Africa during the next 25 years could be over that most precious of commodities – water. Population growth in Egypt is expected to outstrip the water resources of the Nile early in the 21st century. This problem will be greatly complicated by population and economic growth in the upstream nations of Sudan, Ethiopia and Eritrea.'

 For the Nile or any river basin you have studied, **explain** some of the political conflicts which have resulted from controlling the river. **6**

(50)

Map Q3A: River basins of Africa

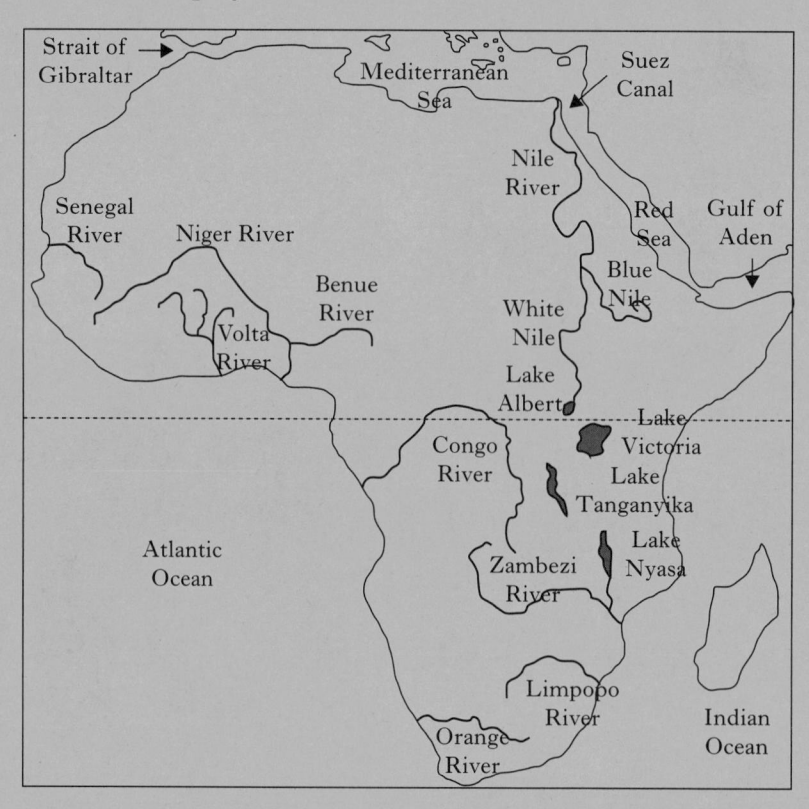

QUESTION 3: continued

Map Q3B: The Nile Basin

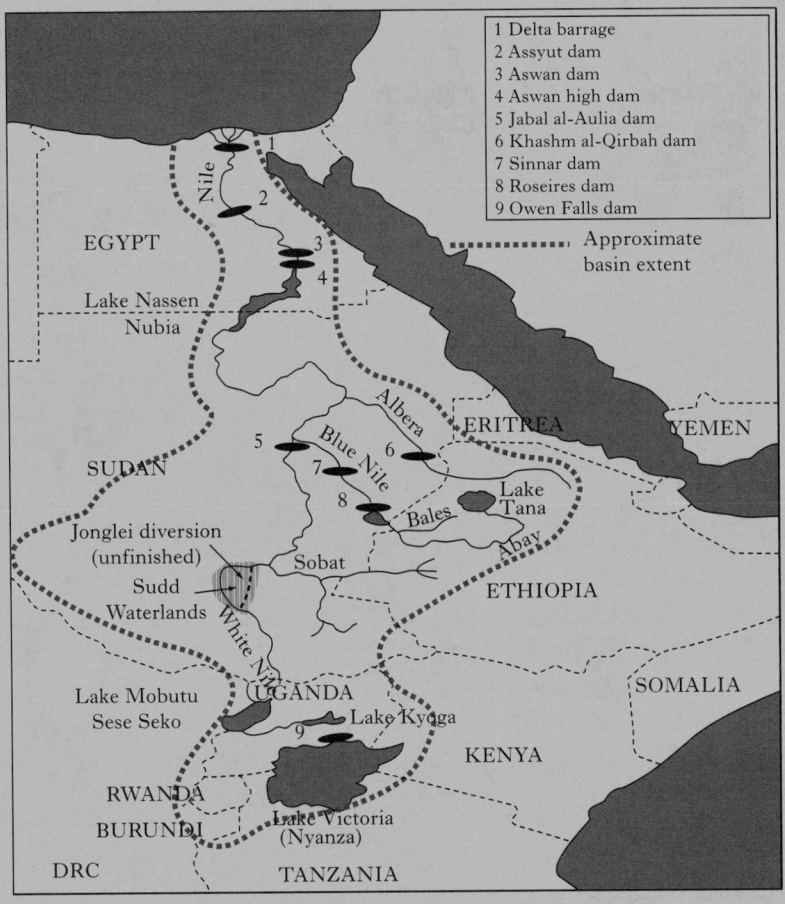

1 Delta barrage
2 Assyut dam
3 Aswan dam
4 Aswan high dam
5 Jabal al-Aulia dam
6 Khashm al-Qirbah dam
7 Sinnar dam
8 Roseires dam
9 Owen Falls dam

▪▪▪▪ Approximate basin extent

Map Q3C: Rainfall in the Nile Basin

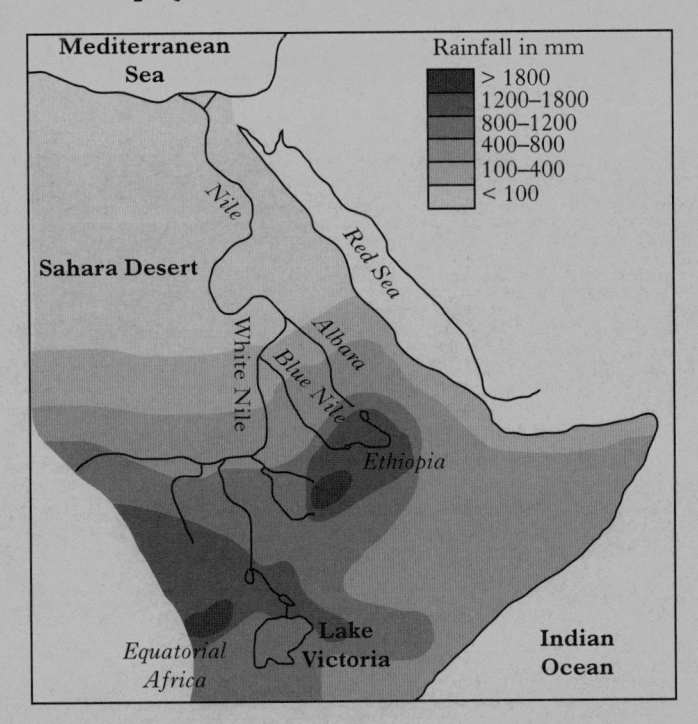

Rainfall in mm
> 1800
1200–1800
800–1200
400–800
100–400
< 100

QUESTION 4: Urban Change and its Management

Marks

(a) 'The initial location of a settlement is influenced by its site. However, even if the site is a good one, the settlement is unlikely to grow into a large city unless it has a good situation.'

For Glasgow, or any other developed world city you have studied, **explain** the ways in which its site and situation contributed to its growth.

8

(b) Study Diagram Q4A.

For the Glasgow Harbour Development, or a specific redevelopment area of a named city in the developed world,

  (i) **give reasons** why this development was needed, and

  (ii) **describe** how the area has changed and evaluate the usefulness of these changes.

16

(c) Look at Diagrams Q4B and Q4C.

Referring to cities you have studied, **give reasons** why the populations of developing cities like Jakarta will continue to grow far more quickly than developed cities like New York.

12

(d) 'Jakarta, Indonesia – Hidden in the alleyways behind Jakarta's fancy malls and in between the high-rise apartment buildings is what Ronny Poluan, a former film maker, calls the "real Jakarta"'.

30 July 2009

Look at the quote and Diagram Q4D.

Describe the social, economic and environmental problems of shanty towns and any advantages shanty towns might have for their inhabitants.

14

(50)

Diagram Q4A: Glasgow harbour

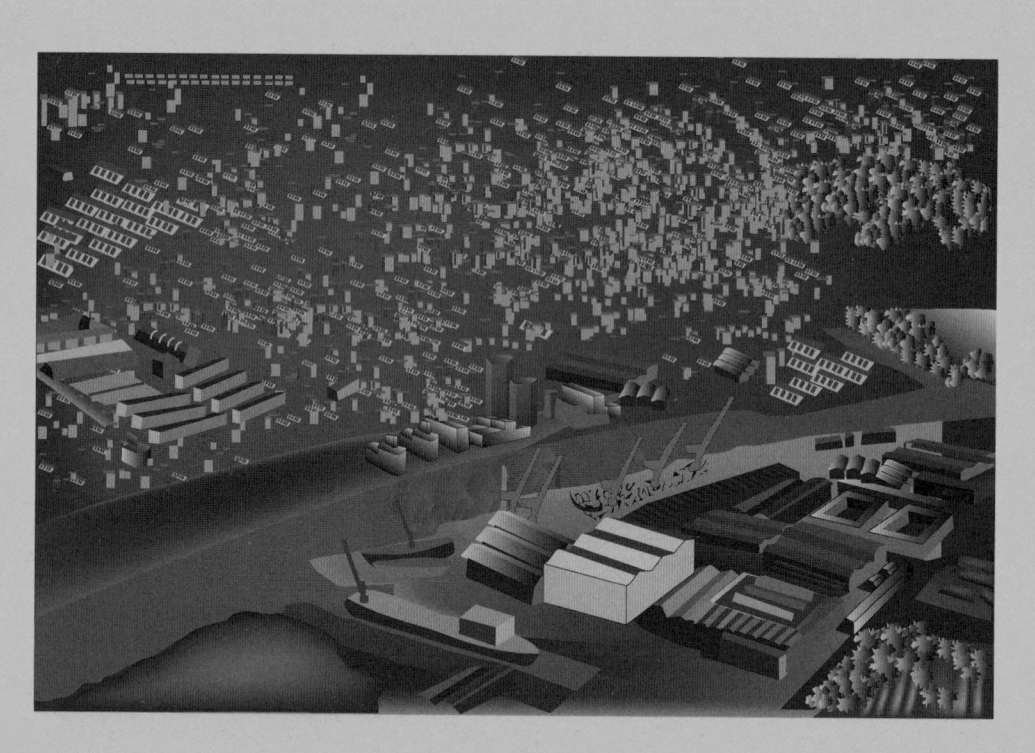

QUESTION 4: continued

Diagram Q4B: Population growth, New York

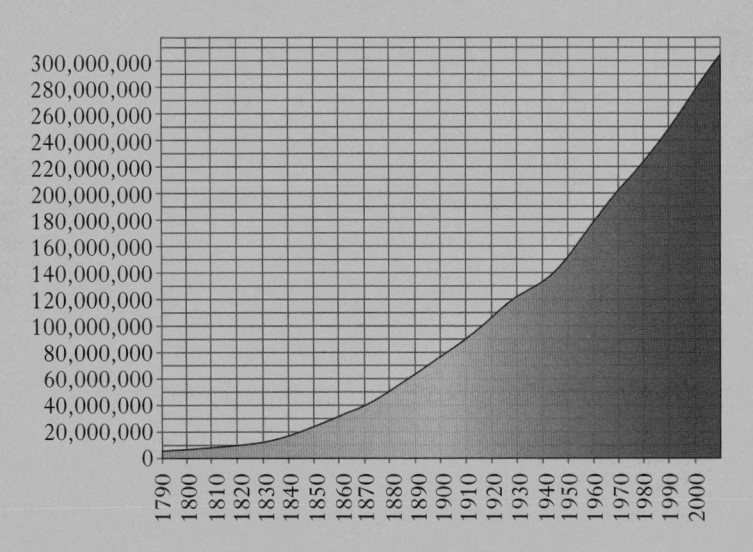

Diagram Q4C: Population growth, Jakarta City, Indonesia

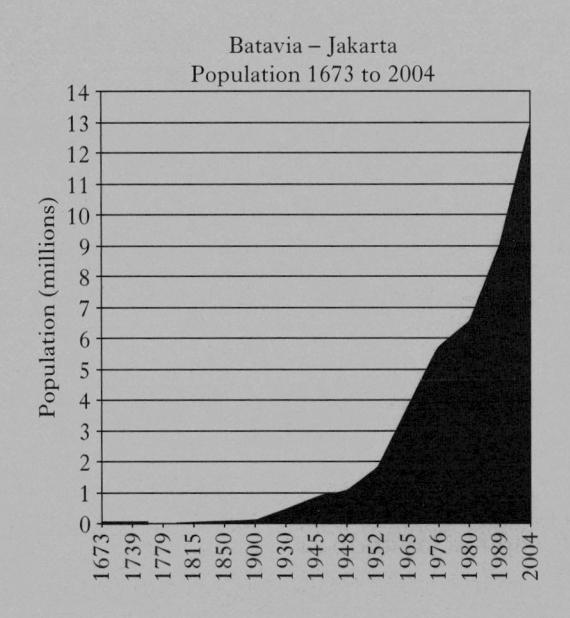

Batavia – Jakarta
Population 1673 to 2004

Diagram Q4D: A shanty town in Jakarta

QUESTION 5: Development and Health

Marks

(a) Composite measures such as the PQLI (Physical Quality of Life Indicator) or HDI (Human Development Indicator) can be used to compare the levels of development between countries.

For **one** of the composite measures above **or** any composite measure you have studied **describe** three of the indicators used and **explain** the usefulness of each indicator.

8

(b) Wide variations in development can exist between developing countries. **Suggest reasons** for this.

You must refer to named examples in your answer.

12

(c) Study Diagram Q5A.

Basic health care in a developing country can be provided through a Primary Health Care programme (PHC). For Malawi, or any other country you have studied, give examples of PHC programmes and **explain** how improving the health of the population can help the country to develop.

10

Diagram Q5A: Population Data for Malawi

Infant mortality per 1000	71
Life expectancy (years)	48
Literacy rates %	72
GDP per capita in US dollars	835
Population living in rural areas %	85
% of population living below poverty line	40

(d) Study Diagram Q5B.

Diagram Q5B shows part of Africa where the population are at risk from malaria.

For malaria or any other water-related disease you have studied,

(i) **describe** measures used to combat the disease.

10

'In Africa today, malaria is understood to be both a disease of poverty, and a cause of poverty.'

Roll Back Malaria spokesperson

(ii) For an area or country you have studied, **explain** why development is hindered by the disease.

10

(50)

Practice Papers for SQA Exams: Higher Geography, Practice Exam 3, Paper 2

Marks

QUESTION 5: continued

Diagram Q5B: Parts of Africa at risk from malaria

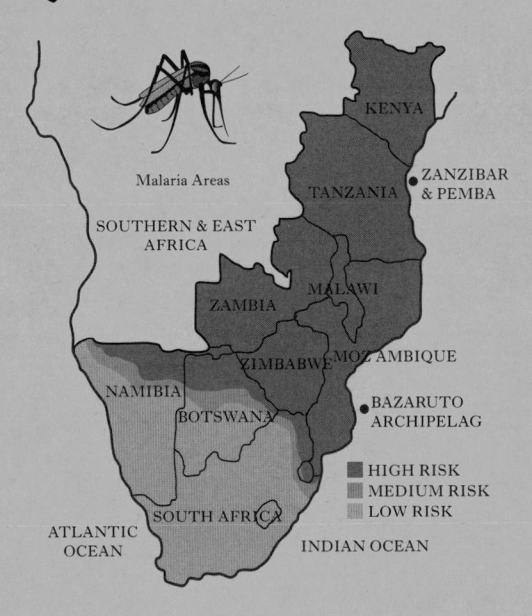

[End of question paper]

Exam 1, Paper 1

> **HINT**
> When answering questions on topics such as the description and explanations of features of carboniferous limestone, the benefits and consequences of river basin management schemes, developmental differences between countries in the economically less developed world and on malaria, good answers will always include reference to a number of named examples.

QUESTION 1: Hydrosphere

(a) **Descriptions may include:**

The River Sowe is in middle or lower course (1).

There are several meanders along the course of the river (1), e.g. at 368779 and 353756 (1). There is also a tributary which joins the river, e.g. 345754 (1). The river is flowing in a south-westerly direction (1) and splits around an eyot at 3540753 (1). The river is quite wide (1).

There is gently sloping land below 70 metres in square 3778 (1) and the land becomes flatter in 3576 (1) with a wide floodplain (1) which is approximately 0·5 km wide in square 3575 (1). In square 3474 the contours are closer together so the river's valley is steeper here (1). **10**

> **TIP**
> You would get 1 mark for specific map evidence, e.g. a grid reference or named feature. For full marks, reference must be made to both the river and its valley.

> **HINT**
> If answering a question on features of coastal erosion, make sure that your answer refers both to erosional landforms and depositional landforms. You should be able to show good knowledge of a range of erosional and depositional processes, not just the names of the processes. If you are asked to explain how a particular feature is formed, such as a meander, a good answer will give a detailed description of how it was formed rather than just describing what happens at a meander. A good answer to a question on the formation of glacial features will also include a range of appropriate diagrams.

(b) **For full marks diagrams must be used.**

Formation of oxbow lake

The water flows faster on the outside bend of a river meander so erodes the banks by the processes of hydraulic action (the sheer force of the water hitting the banks) (2) and by abrasion (where fine materials rubbing against the banks act like sandpaper) causing the banks to become steeper (2). Deposition takes place on the inside bend of a meander where the water is shallower and moving more slowly (1). It has less energy here (1). Over time the neck of the meander becomes more incised and bends back on itself, leaving a very narrow piece of land (1). During a storm or prolonged period of rain, when the river is more powerful, it cuts through the narrow neck and takes a new, straighter route (1). Deposition takes place, leaving the old meander cut off, and an oxbow lake is formed (1). This feature can fill up with sediment and dry out, only filling up after heavy rain (1). **8**

QUESTION 2: Biosphere

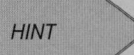

> **HINT**
> You should be able to demonstrate a clear understanding of the relationship between plant species and the dune environment. Answers which discuss climax vegetation should avoid being confined to one kind of environment, such as a dune environment, otherwise fewer marks will be gained.

(a) **Answer might include:**

Plant succession is the replacement over time of the original plants of the area by new plants more suited to the changed conditions of the area (2). The first stage of plant succession is the pioneer stage (1) These are the first plants to colonise an area devoid of vegetation e.g. the slopes of Mt St Helens after the 1980 eruption (1). The roots of these plants find holds in the little soil available and bind it together as well as retaining moisture (2). Pioneers are normally annuals and when they die they add humus to the soil making it more fertile (1). These changes alter the conditions in the area enough to allow other types of plants to move in (1). These plants are bigger and in turn die and increase the nutrients in the soil (1) This then allows perennial plants to move in (1). These plants can now survive due to the increased moisture and nutrients in the soil (1). **6**

QUESTION 2: (continued)

(b) **Allow 1 mark for name of correct species in each location.**

1 Embryo dune

Embryo dunes are found closest to the sea so plant species found here have to be able to withstand strong winds (1) and immersion in sea water (1). There is also a lack of humus (1), so plants such as sea twitch, lyme grass and sea couch are found here (1).

2 Yellow dune

As these plants die, the amount of humus in the soil increases, allowing other plants such as marram grass to colonise the dune (2). The acidity of the soil also increases as these dunes are found further inland (1) and so a greater variety of plants can survive, such as sand fescue and ragwort (1). Marram grass becomes fully established as it can better survive the dry conditions of the dune (1), and its long roots bind the sand together (1). It can also survive being covered in sand. This encourages it to grow more rapidly, thus allowing it to become the dominant species on the dune (1).

3 and 4 Grey dune and dune slacks

At this point the soil becomes much more acidic and has a greater humus content, allowing plants such as red fescue, sea spurge and heathers to survive (2). It is also more sheltered, allowing other species to survive (1). The marram grass dies back (1). Where water accumulates in the slacks, plants such as gorse and bracken can grow (1). Plants can also now gain access to the water table, allowing plants such as cotton grass and alder trees to thrive in the wetter conditions (1). **12**

QUESTION 3: Population

HINT: You should be able to demonstrate a thorough understanding of the links between birth rates, death rates and population change, and the implication of the population structure for countries at various stages of the Demographic Transition Model. When answering questions on a specific type of migration, e.g. forced or voluntary, avoid confusing these with other types of migration such as internal (urban/rural) or introducing irrelevant detail such as 'obstacles to migration' into the answer.

(a) **Answers could include:**

The population pyramid has a wide base, indicating large numbers of children under the age of 15 (1). This means there is a high birth rate for both males and females (1). The pyramid narrows slowly up to the 35–39 age group and then narrows sharply, with very few people over the age of 70 (2). There are more females than males, especially over the age of 65 (1).

The pyramid has a wide base as Malawi is a developing country and the birth rate is high (1). There is a lack of funding for, and knowledge of, family planning and birth control measures, especially in remote rural areas (2). Infant mortality rates are high so more children are born in the hope that some will survive into adulthood (2). Children are also required to work on the land and look after elderly or sick family members (2). The pyramid narrows as a result of poor living conditions (1). Many homes do not have clean running water so diseases such as cholera are common (1). The homes are poorly built and do not have electricity, basic sewerage and sanitation (1). Malawi is a very poor country so there is a lack of money to develop education and health-care programmes (1). If there were more schools and hospitals Malawi would have a skilled labour force which could help them to develop and bring money into the economy which could be spent on improving the standard of living for the people (2). Better health care would increase life expectancy (1). People can be malnourished or not able to grow enough food and are therefore very weak and susceptible to other illnesses, e.g. malaria (1). **10**

TIP: You would receive up to 5 marks for either description or explanation.

(b) **Answers may include:**

In 2029 Malawi's population will have grown (1). The number of children under the age of 15 will have grown significantly, giving the pyramid a very wide base (1). The population in the 35–39 age groups will almost double for both males and females (1). More people over 65 will survive, with life expectancy better for females (2).

As more women of child bearing age will survive, more children will be born (1). Improvements in living conditions, e.g. better housing, better sewerage and sanitation, mean more people will survive (2). Malawi has received a lot of aid from developed countries, e.g. Scotland, and this has helped to develop projects, especially in rural areas (1). More people will have access to clean water as many villages will have wells and water pumps in the centre of them (1). Primary Health Care (PHC) projects will

Worked Answers to Practice Exam Papers Exam 1, Paper 1: Higher Geography

QUESTION 3: (continued)

have been introduced in many rural areas, and they will help to educate locals about the importance of clean water and good sanitation in the prevention of diseases such as cholera and dysentery (2). Farmers will have been shown better ways of farming their land which will help to improve the food supply, therefore improving the people's diet (1). This will make them healthier and more able to work (1). Education programmes for both urban and rural areas will train more teachers and open up more schools, so literacy and numeracy rates will improve and this will help the country to develop a more skilled workforce (2). Through Primary Health Care programmes, families will be educated on disease prevention and will be given simple information to help them stay healthy, e.g. sleeping under insecticide-treated mosquito nets to prevent them from being bitten by anopheles mosquitos (2). More health centres and hospitals will be built and more nurses and doctors will be trained. Therefore more people are surviving (1). **8**

> **TIP**
> You would receive up to 4 marks for either description or explanation.

QUESTION 4: Urban Geography

> **HINT** Answers should refer to a specific city. Named examples are needed for full marks.

(a) **If Glasgow chosen:**

Area A is the Central Business District (CBD). This is the oldest part of the town so many old buildings will be found here, e.g. St Andrew's Cathedral in Clyde Street and the City Chambers at George Square (1). Land is expensive in the CBD so buildings are tall (1) and built close together, with little or no open space (1). Many high order shops are found here as well as the head offices of banks and businesses (1). Only these types of businesses can afford the high rents in this area (1). They also need access to many customers and this is the most accessible part of the city as this is where the main transport routes meet (1). The M8 motorway runs through the city, giving access to many people across the Central Belt (1). The main train and bus stations are found here, e.g. Queen Street, Central Station and Buchanan Street (1) and this allow shoppers and workers easy access to the city centre (1). As the area is easily accessible many offices choose to locate here so areas like Bothwell and St Vincent Streets have old and new office blocks along them (1). The CBD attracts many visitors and tourists, so many hotels are found here, e.g. the Crown Plaza Hotel (1) and different types of entertainment and leisure facilities are found here, e.g. the SECC (1). There is little industry and few housing estates as land values are too high and there is no space for expansion (1); consequently housing is mainly flatted (1). **10**

(b) **Explanations could include:**

Out of town shopping centres, such as Braehead, with lots of parking areas attract many people away from the congested CBD, so causing city centre shops to lose business (2). This results in the closure of some shops, especially on the edge of the main shopping area, as there are fewer people in these areas spending money (2). Empty shops are unattractive and can be broken into or covered in graffiti and this leads to the area looking 'tired' and rundown (2). Out of town centres, such as Braehead in Glasgow, are also under cover, brighter and cleaner than old open city centres, making shopping a more pleasant experience when it is cold, windy and raining (1). They are also accessible to a larger percentage of the population so the town centre can suffer from loss of business, again leading to shop closures and unemployment (1). New shopping areas develop in the CBD to try to keep business there, e.g. Princes Square and Buchanan Galleries have more specialist shops and eating places under cover to try to entice shoppers back into the CBD (2). As the CBD is very accessible to many areas via road and rail it is still popular with many shoppers (1). Out of town centres are more accessible by road but do not always have a rail link close to them. **8**

QUESTION 5: Atmosphere

(a) **Explanations may include:**

Between the equator and the tropics, the sun's rays have less atmosphere to travel through so less energy is lost through atmospheric absorption and reflection (2). The sun's rays strike the area around the centre of the earth at right angles (1) so are more concentrated and there is a net gain of energy (1). At higher latitudes the rays strike the surface at wider angles so surfaces near the equator receive more insolation than the surfaces nearer the poles (1). The insolation striking the equator heats up a smaller surface area than the same amount of insolation at higher latitudes (1). At the tropics, areas of dense

QUESTION 5. (continued)

vegetation such as the rainforest absorb radiation (1), whereas at the poles areas covered in snow ands ice reflect the incoming radiation back into the atmosphere (1).   **8**

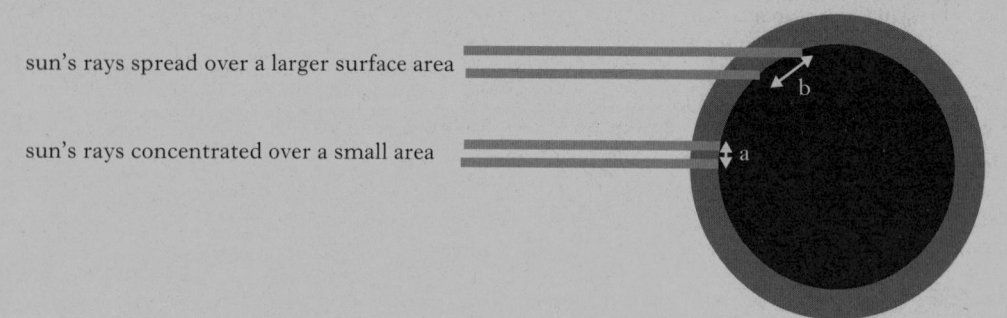

sun's rays spread over a larger surface area

sun's rays concentrated over a small area

(b) **Explanations may include:**

Physical factors which affect changes in global temperatures include changes in the earth's orbit and tilt, which are shown in the Milankovich cycles, and solar activity including sun spot activity, which increases global temperatures (2). Dust and ash from volcanic eruptions can be blown around the world (1), e.g. after the Mount St Helens eruption, and this can block incoming solar radiation (1). Temperatures would then fall below the average (1). Other factors which affect the temperatures are changes in oceanic circulation and local winds, such as El Niño, which can cause temperatures to rise and fall below seasonal averages (2). Retreating ice caps can influence water temperatures and this can affect the earth's albedo (1). In the tundra, areas of rotting vegetation can release gases into the atmosphere and this can affect temperatures (1).   **6**

QUESTION 6: Lithosphere

> **TIP**
> Diagrams should be used to get full marks. You would get up to 2 marks for relevant examples and up to 8 marks for any one feature.

(i) **Swallow holes:**

As limestone is a permeable rock, it allows water to seep through via the joints and bedding planes (1). When a stream flows onto limestone it enlarges the joints over which it flows as a result of chemical weathering (1). Eventually, when a joint has been enlarged sufficiently, the stream will disappear and flow along underground channels, which have been formed by water dissolving the limestone along joints and bedding planes (2). The stream also erodes the channels by the usual process of river erosion as rock debris carried by the river results in vertical erosion (1). The point where a stream disappears underground is called a swallow hole (1). A good example is Gaping Gill in the Pennines (1).

(ii) **Limestone pavements:**

Some areas of limestone were exposed to the elements (e.g. wind and rain) after glaciers passing over the area removed the vegetation and soil covering through abrasion (2). Joints and bedding planes formed in the limestone as it dried out and pressure was released (1). This allowed rainwater to penetrate the limestone (1). As rainwater is weak carbonic acid, it reacts with the limestone as it passes through the rock (1). It dissolves the limestone, through chemical action, enlarging joints and bedding planes (1). On the surface the chemical weathering widens and deepens the joints to form grykes (1). This leaves raised blocks of limestone called clints (1). Water also gets into the joints, freezes at night and widens the grykes (1). An excellent example of a limestone pavement is found at the top of Malham Cove in the Yorkshire Dales (1).

(iii) **Stalactites and stalagmites:**

These form in underground caves and caverns where water seeping into the caves via the joints and bedding planes comes into contact with the air and loses some of its carbon dioxide (1). This makes the water less acidic (1). The water that seeps down through the limestone is loaded with dissolved lime: where the water drips down from a cave roof, a small amount of water will evaporate from each drip and will leave a tiny deposit of lime (2). This is repeated every time water drips from the roof, so that in time a stalactite is formed (1). A stalactite is an icicle-shaped piece of limestone hanging from the ceiling of a cave. In a similar way, lime is deposited on the floor of the cave where the drips land: these deposits build up to form a stalagmite (1). The splash spreads the lime so stalagmites are thicker than stalactites (1). A stalagmite is a stumpy column of limestone sticking up from the floor of a cave. Pillars of limestone form when a stalactite meets a stalagmite (1). Examples of stalactites, stalagmites and pillars can be found in the White Scar Caves, near Ingleton (1).   **14**

Worked Answers to Practice Exam Papers Exam 1, Paper 1: Higher Geography

QUESTION 7: Rural Geography

TIP
Avoid a list as this will only gain 2 marks.

(a) **If shifting cultivation is chosen:**

Shifting cultivation is a type of subsistence farming carried out in areas of rainforest, e.g. the Amazon rainforest of Brazil (1). An area of forest is marked and then burned using a process known as 'slash and burn' (1). Some of the larger trees, especially those bearing fruit, are left as a source of food and to protect the soil (1). They also help aid regeneration of the area (1). The ash from the trees is used as fertiliser (1). The people farm the land using basic tools, such as hoes, as they cannot afford machinery (1). Garden crops such as manioc and cassava are planted in the soil. Heavy rainfall causes leaching and this removes valuable nutrients from the soil (1). As the people cannot afford fertilisers, the soil continues to lose fertility (1). After several years, a new clearing has to be made and the whole process starts again (1). Houses can be in the centre of the clearings and a new clearing will be made adjacent to the original one, meaning that the people usually do not have to move, but in some cases the villagers will move to a new area of the forest altogether (1). The original clearing will be left for many years to allow nutrients to return to the soil and the natural woodland to regenerate (1). This type of farming supports a low population density (1). **8**

(b) In the Amazon rainforest land has also been cleared for settlement, industry and farming. All of these activities have reduced the area of forest available for shifting cultivation (1). However, these activities provide job opportunities for local people (1) and some shifting cultivators have given up and moved into settlements for work or onto cattle ranches or rubber and banana plantations as the jobs provide them with money to support their families (1). Regeneration periods have had to be reduced in some areas due to rises in population and this has led to a decrease in the fallow periods, which has affected soil fertility and also led to a decrease in crop yields (1). Groups such as the Kayapo Indians did not have resistance to Western diseases and many became ill; some also became alcoholics (1). Traditional skills are now being lost as fewer groups are practising this type of farming (1). There have also been conflicts among groups wanting to develop the land and conservationists who want to preserve the rainforest because of its diversity (1). The environment has also suffered as the removal of the trees has led to an increase in soil erosion and leaching (1). This is because the trees provided protection for the soil and the decaying leaf matter added valuable nutrients to the soil (1). The removal of the trees allows the heavy rain to wash away the soils into rivers and this can cause flooding and damage to the landscape (1). Wildlife habitats have been lost and plants used by the locals have been cut down (1). These provided both a food source and cures for simple ailments (1). **6**

TIP
You would get 1 mark for named examples and a maximum of 3 marks for global environmental factors.

QUESTION 8: Industrial Geography

HINT
If asked about location factors in relation to a case study location, you must discuss specific relevant factors rather than industrial location factors in general. When answering a question on a particular industrial concentration, good answers will always include specific reference to named cities/ports/industries/government or EU initiatives/transport links rather than vague references to general location factors. When referring to locations on an OS map, you must be careful to give accurate grid references with eastings before northings.

This area has several car works, e.g. 331809. This is because there is flat, well-drained land in and around Coventry which is good for building on (1), e.g. at 3577 (1). There is open space round the factories allowing room for storage (1) and expansion (1). This is possible beside the car works in squares 3081 and 3476 (1).

Coventry is a large urban area so there is a ready-made workforce available (1) from areas such as Whitmore Park, 330824 and Whitley, 353767 (1). The city will also provide a market for the finished cars (1).

There is an excellent transport network with main roads such as the A444 leading onto one of England's main motorways (1). The M6 is a major link to the north and south of the country (1). The M6 and other motorways can be used to bring raw materials into the works and transport finished vehicles to the larger markets such as Birmingham and London (2). These roads also link Coventry to major ports, such as Hull, Southampton and Dover, allowing cars to be exported to Europe (1). The

QUESTION 8: (continued)

motor works in square 3774 is close to Coventry airport, which can be used to fly in executives and foreign investors for business meetings (1).

This site is outside Coventry so the land will be cheaper and there is plenty of room for expansion and car storage (1). It is also in the countryside so will have an attractive environment (1). **14**

> **TIP**
> You would get up to 2 marks for relevant map evidence, i.e. grid references or names.

Exam 1, Paper 2

QUESTION 1: Rural Land Resources

> **HINT**
> Avoid just listing features. Remember, this answer refers to the Jurassic coastline. Your answer should include the relevant coastal features with specific examples relating to your chosen coastline.

(a) If Jurassic Coast chosen:

Along the Jurassic coast a variety of rock types are found, e.g. chalks and shales (1) These rocks react in different ways to erosion (1): the harder, more resistant rocks form erosional landforms such as headlands, caves, arches, stacks and stumps (2) whilst the less resistant rocks form depositional features such as bays, beaches and spits (2).

A headland is an area of land which juts out into the sea (1) and is surrounded by the sea on three sides (1) Headlands form along coastlines where the land meets the sea at 90 degrees and bands of hard and soft rock are present (2). The coastline is eroded by processes of hydraulic action (1) i.e. the force of water hitting the cliffs (1), corrasion (1) i.e. waves pick up stones and toss them at the cliffs (1), and corrosion (1) i.e. where the rocks are dissolved by sea water (1). The harder, more resistant chalks erode more slowly to form headlands whereas the softer shales erode faster to form bays (2). An example of a headland is the Foreland, near to Studland on the Dorset coast (1).

The headland is continually eroded by the sea and eventually features such as caves, arches, stacks and stumps are formed (1). A small fault or crack in the cliff is attacked by the waves through hydraulic action (1). This crack becomes enlarged and forms a cave (1). Sometimes two caves develop back to back, eventually joining to form an arch (1). An example of an arch is Durdle Door, near Lulworth, Dorset (1). The waves continue to attack the base of the arch through hydraulic action and corrosion (1) and the top of the arch is attacked by weathering processes such as wind, rain and freeze-thaw (1) leaving the top of the arch unsupported. Eventually it collapses under its own weight (1). A tall thin needle-like structure, separated from the headland, is left (1). This is called a stack (1) An example of a stack is Old Harry, north east of Swanage (1) The stack is constantly attacked by the sea and eventually collapses into the sea (1). The feature left behind is called a stump (1). An example of a stump is Old Harry's Wife (1).

Bays are formed where there are layers of hard and soft rock (1). The sea erodes the soft rock much faster than the surrounding hard rock (1). When the sea reaches a another layer of hard rock behind the soft rock, erosion slows down and a bay is formed (1). The eroded cliff rock is broken down and forms new beach material (1). The currents are weaker in bays so beach sediments are deposited (1). A spit is a sand or shingle beach that sticks out into the sea and is joined at one end to the land (1). The main process involved in the formation of a spit is long shore drift (1). This is the gradual movement of material along a beach caused by the waves hitting the beach at an angle (2). **20**

(b) The coastline being looked at is the Dorset coast. Dorset's marine and coastal environments are its main economic and social assets. The natural beauty of this coastline encourages tourism (1). The coastline affords opportunities for cycling, for example along the Purbeck cycle path, for sightseeing or for water activities, such as jet skiing in Eyemouth (2). There are also many clean, safe beaches, some of which have been awarded EU Blue Flag status (1). Other attractions include famous coastal landforms such as Lulworth Cove and Old Harry Rocks (1). The beautiful countryside also attracts many visitors and plays a valuable part in supporting the economy of the rural area (1). The income generated from tourism alone amounted to around £900m in 2008. An average of £30 per person is spent each day by the 17m annual visitors (1). Tourism creates many jobs in hotels, tourist attractions, etc (1).

QUESTION 1: (continued)

Tourism also supports other businesses that supply the tourist industry with goods (1), for example local farmers who sell their produce to restaurants/hotels and boatyards that build and repair the many sail boats used for recreational purposes (1) – this alone brings in over £180m to the economy and employs around 2000 people (1).

Many towns are situated along the coast and the sea provides a livelihood for many people, e.g. fishermen, and there are ferry services to Europe (2). The natural harbours provide safe harbours for importing and exporting goods (1).

The rural area behind Lulworth Cove is used by the Ministry of Defence (1). There are several rifle ranges (1) as well as Lulworth military camp (1).

In social terms, locals get the chance to mix with the visitors and learn about different cultures. This breaks down barriers between people (2). Local people also benefit from the enjoyment of the extra services created for tourists, for example water sports facilities, restaurants, etc (1). Transport into the area might also be improved making for easier journeys for locals (1).

8

> **TIP**
> For full marks both economic and social opportunities should be mentioned. You would get 1 mark for a named example.

(c) (i) **Answers may include:**

The land around this part of the World Heritage Coast is used by a wide variety of people including the Ministry of Defence, the local community, farmers, tourists and conservationists. All these users want to use the area for different activities, which results in conflicts (1).

There can be over 100 000 people visiting this area each year, with 36% visiting during the summer months and over 90% of these arriving by car. This causes conflict with the local community (1). The high number of tourists arriving by car means that traffic congestion is a big problem (1). The car parks at Studland and Lulworth Cove have limited access so there is a concentration of cars in this area (1). Tourists don't always consider where they are parking and can park on grass verges or block exits restricting access for local people and businesses (1). The local people also complain about the noise and litter created by the visitors, which spoil their village and its surrounding environment (1).

The Ministry of Defence uses land behind Lulworth and Studland for training purposes as well as barracks (1). This causes conflicts with the tourists, especially walkers, as the MOD closes roads and coastal footpaths during exercises and the coastline is Dorset's main attraction (2). Access to some beaches is only possible at weekends (1).

There are many important conservation areas here. These include an RSPB reserve, an Area of Outstanding Beauty, Sites of Special Scientific Interest and a Heritage Coastline (1). Conservationists feel that the large numbers of tourists using the area, especially during the summer months, are causing environmental damage (1). The coastal footpaths are being deeply eroded creating eyesores on the coastline (1). Prevention methods can result in access being limited in some places causing conflict with tourists (1).

Farmers also come into conflict with tourists as they walk across farmland, leave gates open and restrict access to fields by irresponsible parking (2).

14

> **TIP**
> You would get 2 marks for named locations of problems or conflict.

(ii) **Answers may include:**

Around the Studland area the four main car parks have been expanded and can now accommodate another 820 cars in an attempt to stop cars parking on grass verges and other inappropriate parking (1). Some paths have been closed to prevent further erosion and sand dunes have been fenced off (1). The fences collect sand where trampling or wind erosion has taken hold (1). Boardwalks are laid along main footpaths to reduce footpath erosion (1). To reduce litter, bins are put along the paths and at the back of beaches (1). Fires are started by irresponsible tourists so fire beaters are available and in some areas fire breaks have been formed (1). The public are being educated on how to look after the environment through the use of leaflets and information boards (1). Rangers are also available to give advice to the public on protection of the environment (1). Organisations like the National Trust and English Nature have take on some of the responsibility for looking after the coastline (1). The money charged by the National Trust for the facilities provided is used to further protect the area and for improvements to the beach and its facilities (1).

8

(50)

Worked Answers to Practice Exam Papers Exam 1, Paper 2: Higher Geography

QUESTION 2: Rural Land Degradation

> **HINT** Answers must include explanations.

(a) If water erosion is chosen:

Erosion by water is the result of rain detaching and transporting soil (1). There are four main processes involved.

Rain splash. This is caused by the impact of raindrops striking the surface of the soil (1). When it rains, water is absorbed by the soil surface and it fills the pore spaces, loosening soil particles and driving them apart (1). The impact of subsequent raindrops hitting the surface splashes soil particles away from the point of impact (1). The effect is to give the soil a pitted surface (1).

Sheet wash. This is when a thin film of water (runoff) transports the soil particles loosened by rain splash by rolling them along the ground (1).

Rill erosion. This is a series of little channels or rills up to 10 cm deep (1). Rill erosion occurs as runoff begins to form small concentrated channels (1).

Gully erosion. Gully erosion results from water moving in rills, which merge together to form large channels (1). Gullies cut deeply into the soil, are several metres in depth and can be permanent (1) **8**

(b) **If the Sahel is chosen:**

Rapid population growth in the Sahel, where most people depend on agriculture for a living, is putting great strain on limited soil and water resources (2). Because of rising population in some of these Sahel countries there is a rising demand for food (1). This then means that any land which is suitable for grazing gets overgrazed (1), which results in the degeneration of the land because of poor agricultural techniques and the lack of vegetation to protect it (2). In most of these countries, because of the rising population, the demand for fuel is also increasing (1). Trees in these areas, once cut down, can't protect the soil, which results in erosion (1). Also, because the numbers of trees are decreasing, animal manure is being used as a fuel. This means that it is not being put back onto the land as fertiliser, which in turn results in poorer land (2). Over-cultivation is a problem. Farmers are forced to grow crops on marginal land (1). The continual use of the soil leads to loss of soil structure, for example in parts of Sudan (1). Nomads have adopted a more sedentary (settled) lifestyle (1) with no change in traditional herding practices, again resulting in over-cultivation of the land, for example in Burkina Faso (1). Slashing and burning of natural forest and bushland have added to the destruction by removing a natural barrier to wind erosion and the root systems that slow topsoil erosion (1). Dust storms have therefore become frequent where the ground has been stripped of vegetation (1). **16**

> **TIP** You would get up to 2 marks for relevant named locations.

(c) One of the consequences of desertification is crop failure. In the Sahel this has led to people being under-nourished and deaths from starvation (1). Famine conditions result, e.g. in Mauritania (1). Mauritania's agricultural zone has also shrunk to a 200 km wide strip (1). When people are under-nourished they are susceptible to diseases such as kwashiorkor (1). Disease and illness become widespread so people cannot work so have no money to buy food (1). They become weaker and a cycle of poverty develops (1). The people in rural areas are forced to leave the countryside and move to the cities in search of food and employment (1). Many of these people cannot find anywhere to live or any employment and end up living in shanty towns on the edge of the city (1). The traditional life of the nomads is under threat as they cannot find food and water for their animals (1). Many are forced to settle in villages or at oases (1). This in turn puts pressure on the surrounding land, leading to over-cultivation (1). In the last 30 years the proportion of Mauritania's people living in the capital Nouakchott rose from 9% to 41%, while the proportion of nomads fell from 73% to 7% (1). Many people are forced to leave their homes and seek food and shelter in neighbouring countries (1). This can lead to conflict with the resident populations (1). International aid is often necessary to ensure the people's survival but this can lead to an over dependence on aid (2). **10**

> **TIP** You would get a maximum of 2 marks for named examples, and 2 marks for description.

(d) (i) In the past the farmers didn't rotate crops, nor did they leave any areas of native grasses; they just dug up everything and planted crops (1). This is no longer the case. The crops are rotated every few years to prevent the same nutrients being removed from the soil and causing infertility (1). Some areas are no longer used to grow crops. They are left under grass (1). In the Plains natural grasses such as clovers and lucerne are planted to increase the nitrogen content, improving the fertility of the land (1). The roots also bind the soil together and stop it being blown away (1). In some areas the crops are cut off a few inches above the ground. The stubble is left standing

Page 90

QUESTION 2: (continued)

in the fields, thus reducing wind and water erosion (2). Later on, it is ploughed back into the ground, improving its fertility (1). In the eastern part of the High Plains terracing and contour ploughing are being used to prevent soil being washed downhill (2). Contour ploughing is the practice of ploughing across a slope following its contour lines (1). The rows formed slow down water runoff during rainstorms, preventing soil erosion and allowing the water time to settle into the soil (2). A terrace is a levelled section of a hill, designed to slow or prevent the rapid surface runoff of irrigation water (1). Trees are planted in rows to stop the wind drying out the ground and blowing the soil away, for example in Oklahoma (1). Strip cultivation is also used (1). This is when small crops are grown between tall crops for shelter (1). In drier areas irrigation is used (1). This keeps the soil moist, allowing crops to grow and preventing soil being blown away (1).

> **TIP**
> For full marks at least four methods should be mentioned. You would get up to 4 marks for specific projects.

(ii) These methods have been successful as there has not been a repeat of the 'Dust Bowl' disaster of the 1930s despite the fact there have been periods of drought (1). For example, in the last decade, parts of Oklahoma and Texas have received 10% to 20% less precipitation than normal (1). Methods such as contour ploughing, shelter belts and planting grasses have been shown to reduce soil erosion by over 50% (1). Trees and plant roots retain water and bind the soil together and successfully prevent soil erosion (1). **16**

(50)

QUESTION 3: River Basin Management

(a) Rainfall in the Damodar Valley is seasonal (1). At some points in the year there is an excess of water, e.g. over 2000 mm in the months of June and July (1). This will lead to the need for flood control (1). Also, reference map Q3B shows that the Damodar river valley is in the area of India which is prone to flooding (1). However, there is very little rainfall between the months of December and March, which will cause drought (1). Since there is an excess of water in the wet season, this could be stored and used in the dry months (1). The temperature graph for Panchet shows constantly high temperatures throughout the year, leading to high evaporation rates (1). Monthly temperatures average around 27° C and are highest when rainfall is lowest (1). The Damodar River has many tributaries, so there is a high drainage density in the river valley, increasing the risk of flooding (1). The amount of water in the river valley can be variable and unpredictable, so planning can help regulate the use and distribution of the water available (1). India's population is rising, so there is a need for a constant supply of water for power supply, domestic use and industrial needs (1). Increasing population means more demand for food supplies, so farmers need a constant supply of water to irrigate their crops during the dry season (1). **10**

> **TIP**
> Up to 4 marks can be gained for using relevant data from the diagrams.

(b) **Physical factors might include:**

The dam should have solid foundations to support its great weight (1). There should be impermeable rock below the reservoir to prevent seepage and water loss (1). There should be enough rainfall/water in the river basin to supply the dams and associated reservoirs (1). The catchment area should have a sufficient flow of water to fill reservoirs (1). The dam should be built at the narrowest point across the river to reduce the length of the dam (1). There should be a large, deep valley to flood behind the dam to allow a reservoir to form (1). The lower the temperature the better, as this will reduce water loss through evapotranspiration (1). If possible, the construction of dams should be avoided in earthquake prone areas (1). The weight of the water stored in the dam can destabilise the underlying strata and cause an earthquake (1). The effect on the hydrological cycle should be considered (1). **10**

> **TIP**
> Both benefits and adverse consequences need to be mentioned for full marks. Answers should refer to the specific river basin chosen. You would get up to 6 marks for appropriate examples.

(c) **Social advantages**

Local populations have improved water supplies leading to better health, with the reduction in water-related diseases like cholera (2). As a result of water being available all year round farmers can grow more crops, leading to increased food supply (1). This can sustain India's growing population (1). The dams provide water for domestic use all year round (1). The production of HEP has increased the supply of electricity to the local populations (1). The dams and reservoirs at Panchet and Mython are being developed for tourist resorts and sightseeing, providing opportunities for locals and visitors (1).

QUESTION 3: (continued)

Social disadvantages

The local people are forced to leave their homes as large areas are flooded behind the dams, forming reservoirs (1). They are resettled in areas which are less fertile and provide a poor livelihood (1). Increase of diseases in irrigation channels (1).

Economic advantages

A more reliable water supply increases crop production, producing a surplus for sale and improving the economy of the country (2). The availability of cheap electricity has encouraged industry to move into the area, allowing the rich minerals of the Damodar Valley to be developed and removed (2). The industry has provided employment for local people, improving the local economy as well as developing the economy of India as a whole (2). The course and depth of the river is more constant improving transport and trade links (1).

Economic disadvantages

The schemes are very expensive to build and maintain (1). In less developed countries money for the river schemes may need to be borrowed and could lead to debt (1). As the river does not flood on a regular basis the silt from the flooded river no longer reaches the fields so there is a greater need for farmers to use fertilisers, increasing costs (2). Roads, etc, can be lost under the newly formed reservoirs, disrupting communications (1).

Environmental advantages

The danger from flooding has been reduced and river flow is reliable throughout the year (1). An increased fresh water supply improves health and sanitation (1). Some people think that the dams and reservoirs are an attractive sight (1). The reservoirs attract wildlife into the area (1).

Environmental disadvantages

High embankments are put in place to control river flow but villages such as Dadpur are constantly under threat of inundation from breaches in these embankments, which could result in the whole village being washed away (2). The frequency of floods has been reduced but they have become much more unpredictable (1). Large amounts of sand and silt are washed down the river, causing soil erosion and silting up of the reservoirs (1). The frequent floods washed away the weeds which clogged the drainage systems, especially in the lower channels of the river (1). The traditional river floods carried large quantities of silt which created fertile growing conditions (1). The incidence of malaria has increased as the breeding grounds are no longer destroyed by the flooding river (1). There is increased water pollution due to all the new industries which have been attracted into the area (1).

24

(d) **Problems may include:**

River basins can cross state or international boundaries, causing difficulties in cooperation between states/countries (1), e.g. the Damodar Valley project needs the cooperation of the governments of several state governments (1). Many arguments occur as to how to divide up the river waters (1). Different states have different laws on water rights (1). The amount of water allowed to reach the lower areas depends on the cooperation of upstream neighbours (1). The quality of the water reaching the lower areas again depends on the water use further up the river (1). The areas lower down the valley can be left with very little, very polluted water due to industrial use further upstream (1). The waters are also used for irrigation, and repeated withdrawal of the river water leads to salinity downstream (1). In some cases the water quality is so poor it needs to be treated, e.g. by desalination plants (1). These are very expensive, and arguments occur as to which state should pay for them (1). **6**

(50)

QUESTION 4: Urban Change and its Management

(a) **Answers may include:**

Urban growth in developed areas is decreasing. This is because of a change in the types and amounts of jobs available (1). For example, in cities such as Glasgow and Newcastle, there has been a decline in traditional industries such as ship building, causing unemployment and a movement of people out of the city (2). There has been an increase in service industry jobs and a growth in out of town shopping centres. The location of these jobs is not necessarily in the city centre (2). Also, nowadays people can work from home (1) or with improved transport systems can commute into the city, so the population drops (1). Many people are moving out of the city looking for larger accommodation, as there is no space for expansion in the city, as well as the peace and quiet of the countryside (2).

In less developed countries more and more people are moving from remote areas, such as the rainforest, into cities such as São Paulo, where there are greater employment opportunities, entertainment, higher wages and better housing (2). This is because, in poorer countries like Brazil, any money available for investment or from overseas aid is put into the city, for example medical care or education (2). People move into urban areas as conditions in the countryside are poor and there is very little employment

QUESTION 4: (continued)

apart from farming (1). Increased mechanisation in farming has taken away the little employment available (1). Life expectancy is low and death rates high as a result of natural disasters such as drought causing crop failure and famine (1). **12**

> **TIP**
> Twelve marks are allocated to part (i). Reference should be made to all three factors. Four marks would be awarded for named examples.

(b) (i) In Rio de Janeiro many hundreds of migrants arrive every day. Most of these new migrants cannot find affordable housing. They are forced to build temporary accommodation, called shanty towns. In Rio de Janeiro these shanty towns are called favelas (1). Houses are made from scrap materials such as wood and metal sheeting (1). Often many, housing does not have services such as sanitation, water or electricity (1). Often many families have to share one tap, there is no sewerage provision, and disease is common (2). Toilets are out in the open, with no treated waste disposal (1). This lack of sanitary conditions causes diseases to spread rapidly (1). In many cases the main sewage drains are open and run through the middle of the settlements (1). In times of heavy rainfall the sewage spills over into the dwellings, creating an ideal environment for disease to spread (1). Many people are unemployed (1). The few jobs which are available are unskilled and poorly paid (1). The high unemployment in the area has led to the growth of the black market and grey economy (1). Another effect of this is the increased trade in drugs, crime and prostitution (1). Rocinha is the largest favela in Brazil, located in the southern edge of Rio de Janeiro (1). It is built on a steep hillside overlooking the city. This land is very unstable and liable to landslides (1). These dwellings are extremely unsightly and, being close to the main tourist beach, cause visual pollution (1). The settlements are usually very overcrowded, Rocinha is home to between 60 000 to 150 000 people (1). There is a lack of services, such as schools and hospitals, so it is hard to break the cycle of poverty (1).

(ii) **Some methods could include:**

The authorities in Rio de Janeiro have taken a number of steps to reduce problems in favelas. They have set up self-help schemes (1). The local authority provides local residents with the materials needed to construct permanent accommodation, including breeze blocks and cement (1). The local residents provide the labour. The money saved can be spent on providing basic amenities such as electricity, water and perhaps a school (2). Today, almost all the houses in Rocinha are made from concrete and brick (1). Roads have been built to improve communications into Rocinha. Parts of Rocinha are accessible by bus (1). The authorities have also set up a small number of health clinics to allow basic health care and provide at least one gynaecologist and two paediatricians (1). Standpipes have been introduced to provide a basic water supply, even in the poorest areas (1). The permanence of Rocinha is now accepted by the Brazilian government, despite the fact that the land was initially occupied illegally (1). Basic infrastructure has been provided and Rocinha has become an area of permanent settlement, integrated into the formal city through the legalisation of some land holdings (1). **18**

> **HINT** Avoid generalised answers: your answer should be specific to a chosen city.

(c) **Conflicts**

London's rural–urban fringe is characterised by a mixture of land uses, most of which require large areas of land (1), for example the Chessington World of Adventures theme park and Epsom, a major horse-racing course, as well as retail parks, business parks, waste disposal sites and a wide range of residential areas (2). These different land users all have different needs, therefore conflicts occur (1).

There is a growing demand for land to be released to meet the demand for suburban residential housing (1). This land can only be found at the rural-urban fringe, so this means that there could be a loss of farmland (1). Farmers also complain about vandalism to their property coming from the nearby housing estates (1). The country park and golf courses close to Epsom Common are also in danger of being swallowed up as London expands and more land is needed for housing (1).

The rural–urban fringe has become an increasingly popular area for economic developments (1). Competition for land in these areas increased significantly during the 1990s. The land is much cheaper here than in the city centre, and many factories that were once in inner city locations have moved to these areas as their previous locations lacked space for expansion (2). This again can cause conflict with farmers and residents (1).

High land values in the city centre and traffic congestion have led to the development of out of town shopping centres. These areas need large amounts of land for parking as most people arrive by car (2). As car ownership increases there is an increased demand for new/improved transport links (1). By-passes, ring roads and new motorways require large amounts of land around cities, for example the M25 ring road around London (1).

QUESTION 4: (continued)

There is increasing pressure from environmental groups to restrict urban sprawl and protect the environment on the edge of cities from economic pressures (1). If urban sprawl continues unchecked, many wildlife habitats would be destroyed (1). Conservationists and farmers want to protect nature reserves and farmland but open space for recreation is required by people living in the nearby urban area (1).

> **HINT**: You need to make some comment on the success of the strategies.

Strategies

One strategy is the creation of a greenbelt (1). Planning permission is not usually granted for schemes on greenbelt land, although there is often great pressure to allow proposals to go through (1). However, their success is limited as greenbelts are being breached constantly, for example the M25 is built through much of London's greenbelt (1). One of the main problems of greenbelts is that they have led to people commuting further in to work (1). Since developers cannot get planning permission to build on the greenbelt they move even further out, affecting more rural land (1). Although greenbelts have stopped unregulated growth, their success is limited (1).

Local authorities have tried to solve these conflicts by having strict guidelines to control further developments in the urban–rural fringe (1). They can give permission if the development is for the 'common good', for example a new housing development was given permission to be built on the greenbelt at the old Epsom Hospital cluster (1). This has been effective – housing was provided but also it improved the environment by providing garden and recreational facilities for the local population (1).

Developers are being encouraged to develop brownfield sites instead of greenfield sites as well as renovating older inner city property to reduce the need for new housing (1). This has reduced the amount of building taking place on the fringe (1). **20**

(50)

QUESTION 5: Development and Health

> **HINT**: The best answers will show a good understanding of why a country is at a particular stage of development by explaining the impact of different factors, such as industrial output, resources, social factors such as birth and death rates, levels of medical and education provision, etc, rather than simply giving a single reason for one or more countries from a memorised list. If you are asked to discuss environmental problems in ELDC cities, make sure that your answer relates to a variety of problems and does not focus solely on one problem such as 'shanty towns' or 'pollution'. If the question provides data on a number of countries or cities, do not refer to these if your knowledge is minimal. Refer instead to a country or city which you have studied and of which you can provide specific details.

(a) South Korea is a Newly Industrialised Country (NIC) and has the highest GDP and life expectancy. Its infant mortality rates are also lower than the other countries shown (1). This is because South Korea has attracted foreign investment (1). Multinational companies are attracted to South Korea because it has an educated, cheap workforce, flat land for factories and natural harbours with deep, sheltered waters to trade from (2). The money earned from industry and exports can be spent on education and health care, improving infant mortality rates and life expectancy (1). The country's infrastructure can also be improved and this attracts more companies so the country becomes wealthier and people's standard of living improves (1).

India has a large population and this can hinder development as it puts a great strain on the country's resources (1). Many people are subsistence farmers and do not show up in economic statistics (1). There is a lack of money for education and health care, especially in rural areas, and many diseases exist which contribute to the high infant mortality rates and lower life expectancy (2).

Sierra Leone is one of the world's poorest countries and has suffered from political instability and civil war (1). This means that money which could be spent on improving education and health care is being spent on arms and ammunition (1). People's lives are being affected and farms cannot grow food to feed the people (1). Many people are displaced and become refugees (1). Foreign countries will not invest in these areas so the country fails to develop and this leads to a low GDP (1). The country will not receive a lot of aid as the donors feel that the aid will be diverted and not reach the people who need it most; donors fear that the money will be spent on arms and ammunition instead of food, education and health care (2). **10**

> **TIP**: You would get up to 3 marks for specific, relevant examples. Avoid generalised answers.

> **HINT**: Your answer must refer to a named country.

QUESTION 5: (continued)

(b) Primary Health Care (PHC) strategies have been introduced by many developing countries in an effort to improve the health of the population. In rural areas of China, the 'barefoot doctors' programme has been introduced (1). Barefoot doctors are local people who are given basic training so that they can attend to their communities' health needs (1). They treat simple ailments, from snake bites to appendicitis (1). This means that medical aid is available within easy reach of the community and this saves people from travelling to the nearest hospital (1). It also takes pressure off the large hospitals, allowing them to deal with more serious illnesses (1). The barefoot doctors are effective as they provide hope of health care for people in more remote areas where budgets and manpower can be limited (1). Training costs are low. In India it costs about $100 to train a health worker for a year (1).

On the other hand, despite the success of barefoot doctors, there are not enough of them to care for everybody and some lack the medical skills required, which can lead to inappropriate prescribing of drugs and incomplete surgery (2). Also, the system often breaks down if funding is no longer available for further training (1).

Although barefoot doctors cannot carry out major procedures, they can provide people with important information and services (1). They can provide families with advice on birth control, vaccinations and basic hygiene (1). These things will help prevent the spread of disease, reduce birth rates and infant mortality rates (1). As well as giving out advice the medics can visit those sick people who are too ill to travel to the nearest hospital. They can also run clinics in the larger villages and take a mobile health van to more remote villages (2). The advantage of this is that they are well known and trusted by villagers to provide them with vital health care (1). If the cases are too complex they are referred on to the nearest hospital. This is where highly trained doctors and nurses can provide a wider range of facilities and medical care (2). These hospitals are very effective, as they provide a good standard of medical care and money is invested in them by local governments (1). PHC programmes are also trying to provide villages with local dispensaries. This gives the people access to essential modern drugs, traditional remedies and family planning (2).

Organisations are also looking into how they can improve the sanitation facilities and the amount of clean drinking water available to people in rural areas, as improvements in these areas would lower the cases of cholera and malaria (2). If people were healthier they would be more able to work and provide for their families (1). **10**

> **HINT** Your answer needs to cover both human and physical conditions to gain full marks.

(c) (i) Malaria is found in humid, tropical areas of the world where temperatures range from 15–40 degrees centigrade (1). The rainfall provides areas of stagnant water for the female anopheles mosquito to lay her eggs (1) and high temperatures provide the ideal temperatures for them to hatch (1). There needs to be vegetation such as trees and bushes to provide shade for the mosquitoes to digest their blood meal (1). Humans provide the mosquitoes with their blood meal (1) and their homes provide them with shade to digest their blood meal (1). Utensils and empty buckets left outside homes catch stagnant water and this provides more breeding grounds as mosquitoes require very little water to lay their eggs (1). Poor sewerage and sanitation, as well as irrigation channels and paddy fields, can also provide areas of stagnant water (1). **6**

> **HINT** For full marks, evaluation is needed.

(ii) and (iii) **Prevention methods and success**

Draining areas of stagnant water, such as puddles and swamps, can reduce the number of breeding grounds for the mosquitoes to lay their eggs (1). However, in tropical areas there can be heavy rainfall every day so new areas of stagnant water can appear all the time (1). This method can be very time-consuming and would need to be done every day (1).

Spraying insecticides such as DDT (now banned) on breeding grounds and in people's homes killed the mosquitoes and their larvae (1). This was easy to do but had to be done thoroughly to be effective and over time mosquitoes have developed resistance to the insecticide (1). DDT is also harmful to the environment (1). Newer insecticides, such as malathion, have been developed (1). As this is petrol-based it is less harmful to the environment but homes and breeding grounds have to be sprayed more frequently and this makes it expensive to do (2). It also stains the walls of people's houses a horrible yellow colour (1) and villagers complain about the smell, so some don't want it sprayed in their homes (1).

Egg whites can be sprayed on the stagnant water to suffocate the larvae by clogging up their breathing tubes so that they drown (1). This works, but in areas where food is scarce it is a waste of a valuable food source and only the whites are used, so the yolks can be wasted (1). This would need to be done frequently and requires a plentiful supply of eggs (1).

A newer method is to impregnate coconuts with Bti bacteria (1). After a few days the fermented coconuts can be broken open and thrown into mosquito-infested ponds. The larvae eat the coconuts and the bacteria destroy their stomach linings (1). This is a cheap and environmentally friendly way to reduce the number of mosquitoes as the bacteria will not harm humans or the environment (1). Coconuts grow well in tropical areas and two or three coconuts will 'control' a small pond for 45 days (1).

One successful way of controlling the spread of malaria near human settlements in SE Asia is to add fish to the water in paddy fields, as they eat the larvae, so people working in the fields are less at risk of catching malaria (1). The fish are easy to breed and a vital source of protein for the people (1).

Drugs can also be given to people to stop them catching malaria or to treat malaria sufferers (1). Chloroquine is cheap to produce but in recent years mosquitoes have become immune to it so it is now less effective (1). It has to be taken properly to be effective and can be expensive for people in poor countries such as Malawi (1). Malarone is a newer drug and it is safe to give to children. It is around 98% effective and has virtually no side effects (1). Another newer drug, quinghaosu, first discovered in China from the artemisia plant, is now being developed and initial trials have shown that it is effective in helping malaria sufferers (1). Vaccines are being trialled in places such as Colombia and Gambia, but they are still at the trial stage (1). Vaccines would be easy to administer through PHC schemes and if given to children would reduce the incidence of malaria and reduce infant mortality rates in many areas (2).

Education is an effective, simple and cheap way of tackling malaria when done through primary health care programmes (1). People can be given advice which helps prevent them catching malaria (1). An effective yet simple way is to sleep under an insecticide-treated bed net (1). Mosquitoes are most active between dusk and dawn and nets protect children and adults while they sleep. These nets cost about £5 and will stop people being bitten (2). Villagers should also be encouraged to screen doors and windows to stop mosquitoes entering their houses (1). People should also be told not to leave buckets, etc, upturned as they provide breeding grounds for mosquitoes to lay eggs in (1). People can also use sprays and creams such as Autan which can be put on the skin to stop people being bitten (1). Visitors and locals can also take anti-malarial drugs, but they are expensive and have to be taken correctly to work properly (1). Most groups like the World Health Organisation and the Roll Back Malaria group realise that eradication of the disease is very difficult, but the measures outlined should help to reduce the number of people contracting and dying from malaria (1). **24**

(50)

Exam 2, Paper 1

QUESTION 1: Atmosphere

> **HINT**: When answering this question you should be able to name and identify the characteristics of two air masses. Poor answers often fail to give specific detail in their identification of source areas of air masses. It is not enough to give vague comments such as 'formed over the sea' or 'over the land'.

(a) A tropical maritime air mass originates in tropical latitudes over the Atlantic Ocean (1). It brings warm, moist, unstable air (1). It is moist, as it has travelled across the ocean, picking up moisture as it moves (1). Since it originates in tropical latitudes it brings hot/very hot conditions (1). A tropical continental air mass originates over the land, e.g. the Sahara Desert (1), in tropical latitudes (1). It brings warm, dry, stable conditions as it travels over land as opposed to water (1). In both summer and winter it brings hot/warm and dry conditions (1). **8**

> **TIP**: For full marks, reference should be made to both air masses.

(b) Lagos, on the south coast, has rainfall for twelve months of the year (1). It has a far higher rainfall total than both Jos and Timbuktu (1). There are two distinct rainfall peaks in June and October (1). Jos is located between Lagos and Timbuktu and has little rainfall from November to March (1). From April to October there is a marked wet season, with the highest rainfall in July and August (1). Timbuktu is in the north and is the driest of the three places, with almost no rainfall between October and May (2). The little rain it gets falls between June and September, with a maximum of 82 mm in August (2).

The reason for these differences is the result of the movement of the ITCZ (Inter Tropical Convergence Zone) (1). As Lagos is at the coast it is influenced by tropical maritime air which brings warm, wet conditions (2). This is the reason for its high annual rainfall total (1). The twin peaks in June and October are the result of the ITCZ migrating northwards then southwards later in the year as it follows the midday sun (2). As Jos is north of Lagos it is influenced by tropical continental air for five months of the year (1). As the ITCZ migrates north it brings wetter weather associated with the tropical maritime air mass (1). This accounts for the heavy rainfall between April and September (1). Timbuktu is much further north and affected by the hot, dry tropical continental air mass for most of the year (1). The ITCZ, pulling in the wetter tropical maritime air, in most years does not reach this far north, meaning little or no rainfall for Timbuktu (2). **10**

> **TIP**: You would get up to 4 marks for description, 1 mark per valid point and 2 marks for an extended point.

QUESTION 2: Lithosphere

> **HINT**: Answers should provide a full description of glacial features specific to Braemar, identifying and naming appropriate examples from the map with appropriate grid references.

(a) As ice moves across an area it erodes the landscape. On the map extract there are several corries, such as Coire nan Clach in grid square 0900 and Coire na Cichie (1) in 0998 (1). Some corries are occupied by small lakes or lochans, such as the one found in grid square 0990 (1) called Dubh Lochan (1). An arête, which is a steep, narrow ridge which separates two corries, can be seen at 095995 (1). There are also U-shaped valleys on the map which were carved out of the landscape by large glaciers which occupied V-shaped river valleys (1). Smaller valleys join the main valley in squares 1191 and 1591 (1). The River Dee is an example of a misfit stream (1) which flows across the main valley floor, for example at 125906 (1). There are several hanging valleys. These were tributary valleys occupied by smaller glaciers so less erosion took place (1). An example of a hanging valley can be found at 134996 (1). There are also examples of truncated spurs, such as the one found at 146980 (1). This was an interlocking spur which was blunted by a glacier eroding it (1). **8**

> **TIP**: You would receive up to 2 marks for grid references or named examples.

Worked Answers to Practice Exam Papers Exam 2, Paper 1: Higher Geography

QUESTION 2: (continued)

> **HINT** — For the chosen features, the processes involved in their formation must be explained. A sequence of fully annotated diagrams could achieve full marks.

(b) **Formation of a corrie**

Corries form when snow collects in hollows, especially in the shaded northern sides of a mountain. The snow becomes compressed, turning into ice or neve and begins to move downhill because of gravity (1). Freeze-thaw weathering takes place at the back of the hollow (1). This is where water gets into cracks in the rock and freezes at night, putting pressure on the rock which eventually cracks (1). Plucking occurs (1) where the ice sticks to the rock and pulls it away as it moves and steepens the back wall (1). Material which falls into the glacier sticks to the ice and causes abrasion on the floor of the hollow (1) as the material acts like sandpaper, smoothing and deepening the hollow to form a deep rock basin (1). Rotational slip erodes the middle of the hollow and a shallow rock lip forms (1). As the glacier moves out of the hollow it loses some energy and material is deposited on the rock lip (1). When the ice retreats and melts, a steep, deep armchair-shaped hollow is left (1). Water can gather in the bottom of the hollow, forming a small corrie lake or tarn (1).

Formation of a truncated spur

A truncated spur is the result of glacial erosion along a pre-glacial valley (1). Before the ice age the river flowed round interlocking spurs (1). A glacier flowed down the valley eroding the landscape through the processes of plucking and abrasion (1). This straightened and deepened the valley as large masses of solid rock were eroded, leaving steep cliffs known as truncated spurs (1). **10**

QUESTION 3: Rural Geography

(a) **If intensive peasant farming is chosen:**

This type of farming is found in South and South-east Asia in areas with a monsoon climate, e.g. in India and Thailand (1). A small area of land is intensively farmed. Terraces are built into the hillside in some areas to increase the amount of land which can be farmed (1). Bunds, which are embankments made of soil, are used to divide the fields (1). Rice is the main crop grown. It is mainly grown on river plains and deltas because, when the river floods, it will provide water and nutrients for the soil, e.g. along the Lower Ganges Valley in India (2). The land may need to be irrigated in the drier season, especially if some wheat is being grown (1). This type of farming is mainly subsistence and requires many workers (1). Water buffalo or oxen are used to plough the fields as the people cannot afford machinery (1). The manure from the animals is used as fertiliser, as artificial fertilisers are too expensive (1). Rice seeds are planted in nursery beds and then transplanted into the paddy fields as seedlings (1). Rice is harvested by hand using sickles or knives (1). Villages tend to be nucleated, to leave as much room for crops as possible (1). These are close to the paddy fields. Some trees will be planted to provide shelter for crops, prevent soil erosion and provide the villagers with fruit (2). **10**

> **TIP** — You would get up to 4 marks for description, 1 mark per valid point, and 2 marks for an extended point.

> **HINT** — When answering questions on this topic, good answers will refer to changes that can be described as 'new' and 'continuing'. If asked to discuss the causes and impact of change in a given system, good answers will avoid simply describing the changes based on the information provided in the diagram.

(b) **Likely recent changes in farming practices to have taken place could include:**

The Green Revolution was introduced in Asia to try to increase food production as the population was growing rapidly (1). The land was reformed. Farms were consolidated to make fields larger (1). This helped to increase yields and make it easier for machines (1). However, many farm labourers lost their jobs and had to migrate to the large towns and cities to find work (1). As they had few skills, many of them ended up living in the shanty towns (1). The natural look of the area was lost and soil erosion became a problem in some areas (1). New varieties of seeds were introduced to give better yields, e.g. new varieties of rice, maize and wheat (1). This allowed surplus crops to be sold, bringing in money which could be used for new seeds and equipment (1). More food was available to feed the growing population in countries like India and Thailand. This helped to keep them healthy and fit for work (1). However, many of the locals did not like the taste of the new crops and food was wasted or fed to animals instead (1). Fertilisers and irrigation systems were introduced and this improved yields (1). These are expensive and many of the poorer farmers could not afford them so went out of business (1). The fertilisers and pesticides were also harmful to the environment and some were washed into the river systems, polluting the water (1). Irrigation during the drier months meant that more water was used, leaving less for drinking and cooking (1). It can also lead to salinisation in the soil (1). Machines allowed tasks to be completed quickly, but these are expensive to buy and maintain (1). Many farmers had to borrow money to buy the machines, putting them into debt (1).

Worked Answers to Practice Exam Papers Exam 2, Paper 1: Higher Geography

QUESTION 3: (continued)

Farmers could not fix them when they broke down and some could not afford to buy fuel (1). Some farmers resorted to the older ways and could not compete with the richer farmers, so lost out on selling their crops (1). Other farmers could not pay back their loans and were forced to sell their farms to the richer farmers in order to pay back the money they owed (1). Communications were improved in areas, making them more accessible and making it easier for farmers to transport goods to markets (1). **8**

> **TIP**
> Answers should be explanations.

QUESTION 4: Industrial Geography

(a) In South Wales there were raw materials for the making of steel. For example, coal, iron ore and limestone were all available in the valleys and were easy to extract (2). There was flat land in the valleys for building collieries and factories (1), e.g. along the Rhondda Valley (1). The flat valley floors allowed for railway lines to be built along them and these were then used to transport the bulky raw materials (2). The railway lines linked the coal mines with the factories and with the ports (1). Cardiff and Swansea both had deep, sheltered water so they developed as ports which exported the coal and iron ore to the other heavy industries in the UK and to places in the British Empire (1). There were markets for the raw materials in England, e.g. Sheffield (1), and abroad in countries like India (1). Settlements provided a ready work force (1) and people moved for work from rural areas into the mining areas, e.g. Ebbw Vale, and into the steel making area of Port Talbot (1). **10**

> **TIP**
> You would get up to 1 mark for named relevant examples.

(b) The raw materials of coal, iron ore and limestone became more difficult to extract as miners had to mine deeper underground for supplies, e.g. in Torfaen and Powys (1). This is expensive but also more dangerous so some mines closed as there were not enough supplies to merit the expense of extraction (1). In some areas the raw materials ran out all together so the collieries had to be shut down (1). Other industrial areas, like the Ruhr in Germany, had large reserves of the raw materials and large amounts of it were easy to extract, so South Wales lost orders (2). Mines closed as a result of this competition from abroad (1).

There was a lack of flat land, the valley floors were quite narrow, so expansion was restricted and there was very little room for larger factories and storage areas (2). Newer materials such as aluminium were being manufactured and, as aluminium is lighter and does not rust, demand for steel dropped (1). As the orders dropped, more factories closed and more people lost their jobs (1). Colombia, Germany and Japan were producing steel more cheaply so this also led to orders being dropped (1).

With the closure of the mines and steelworks the environment improved (1). There was less air pollution as coal was not being burned, so carbon dioxide emissions were reduced (1). The air became cleaner and industrial waste was no longer being dumped in the streams and rivers so there was less water pollution (1).

However, derelict buildings became an eyesore and were dangerous (1). People dumped rubbish and unwanted household goods in the area and it became even more unsightly (1). The waste products piled up in the bings leached into the soil, causing contamination (1). **8**

QUESTION 5: Hydrosphere

(a) **Descriptions may include the following points**

The river flows in a north-easterly direction to 156927 then in a south-easterly direction to point 190907 (1). The river is quite narrow at 100895 and is much wider at point 190907 (1). The river flows slowly over a wide, flat floodplain, for example at 125913 (1). The river is prone to flooding and this is evident in grid square 1391, where there is marshland and in grid square 1592, where there are embankments (1). There are several meanders, with a large incised meander (1) at 177919 (1). Several tributaries join the river between these points and two have their confluences at 123906 and 148925 (1). Braiding can also be found at several points with eyots or islands present at 112900 and 154927 (1). The river flows through a U-shaped valley and has steep sides, especially to the north at 105903 and 130921 where the contours are very close together indicating high, steep land (1). The valley at 135908 and 173923 is gentler as the contours are more widely spaced (1). The flat valley floor is approximately 0·5 km wide in grid square 1089 widening to 1 km wide in grid square 1491 (1). **8**

> **TIP**
> You would get up to 1 mark for specific map evidence, for example grid references or names.

QUESTION 5: (continued)

HINT: Annotated diagrams should be used. Answers without diagrams would only receive a maximum of 5 marks out of the 6 available.

(b) Waterfalls are found where hard rock such as limestone overlies softer rock such as mudstone (1). The water is powerful and erodes the softer rock by hydraulic action (1) (the sheer force of the water hitting off the rock) (1). A plunge pool forms. The softer rock is worn away and the hard rock is undercut (1) and an overhang of hard rock is left suspended above the plunge pool (1). This collapses as there is nothing to support it and the rock falls into the plunge pool (1). Rock fragments swirling around deepen the plunge pool (1). This process is repeated over a long period of time and the waterfall retreats upstream leaving a steep-sided gorge (1). A good example of this can be found at High Force on the River Tees (1).

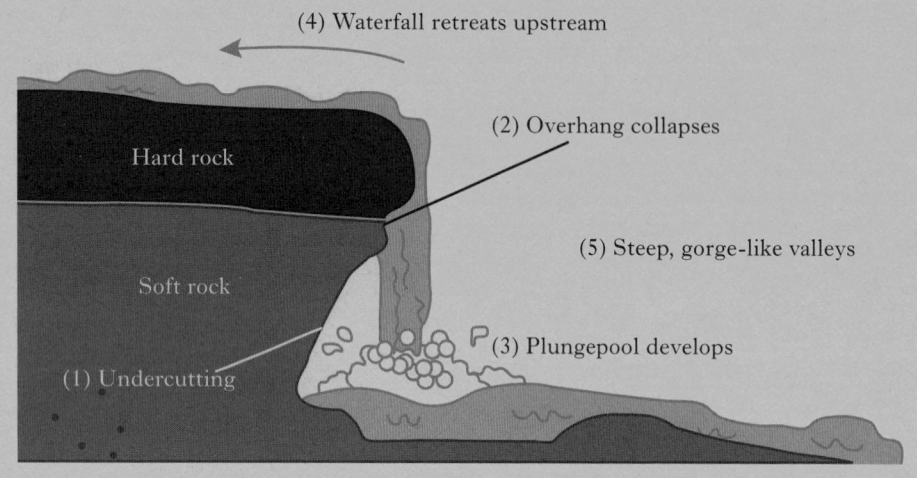

Diagram annotations:
- (4) Waterfall retreats upstream
- Hard rock
- (2) Overhang collapses
- (5) Steep, gorge-like valleys
- Soft rock
- (3) Plungepool develops
- (1) Undercutting

FORMATION OF WATERFALL

QUESTION 6: Biosphere

HINT: The diagram should have annotations.

(a)

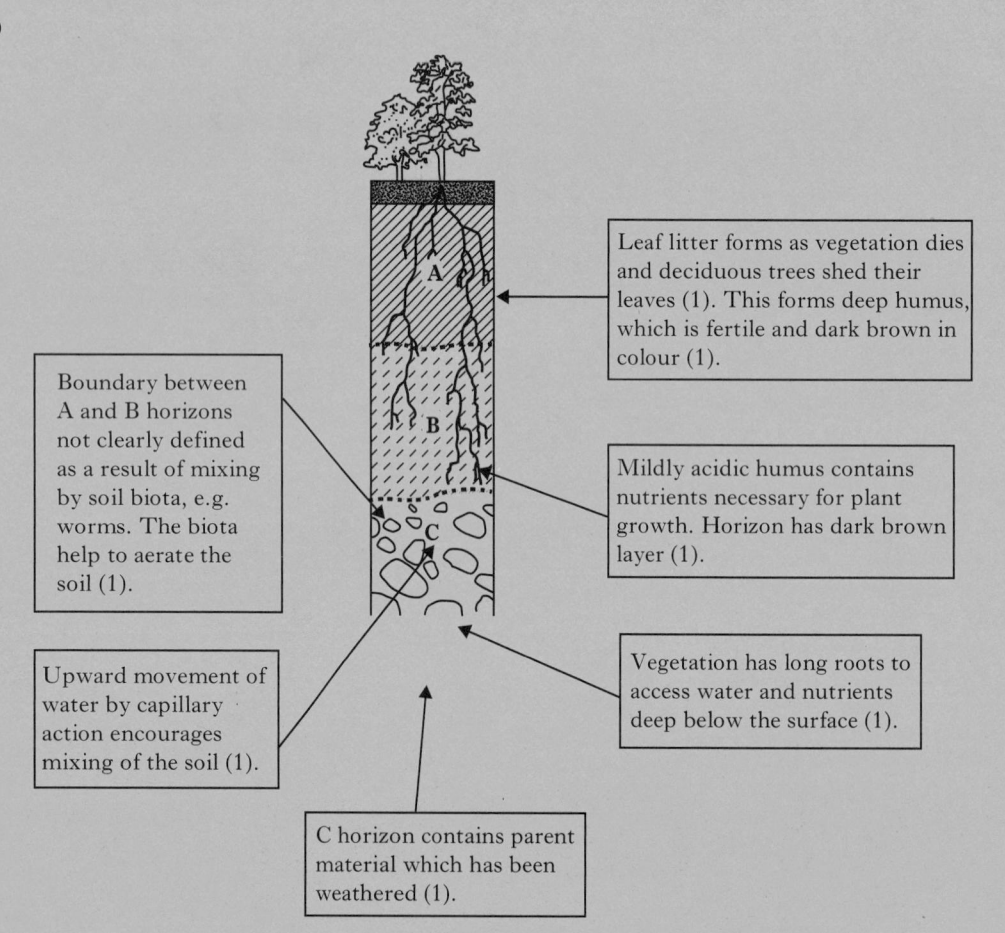

Diagram annotations:
- Leaf litter forms as vegetation dies and deciduous trees shed their leaves (1). This forms deep humus, which is fertile and dark brown in colour (1).
- Boundary between A and B horizons not clearly defined as a result of mixing by soil biota, e.g. worms. The biota help to aerate the soil (1).
- Mildly acidic humus contains nutrients necessary for plant growth. Horizon has dark brown layer (1).
- Upward movement of water by capillary action encourages mixing of the soil (1).
- Vegetation has long roots to access water and nutrients deep below the surface (1).
- C horizon contains parent material which has been weathered (1).

QUESTION 6: (continued)

(b) **For brown earth soil the following points could be included in your answer:**

Brown earth soils are found in temperate areas of the world. The thick humus layer is formed from decaying leaves, e.g. from deciduous trees like the horse chestnut and oak, which shed their leaves in the autumn (2). The organic material decays well in the warm climate, adding humus to the soil (1). The long tree roots go deep into the soil, allowing the minerals to be moved about and recycled (1). There is a little leaching of the soil as precipitation is slightly greater than evapotranspiration (1). This leaching of the minerals can cause the development of an iron pan (1), which hinders drainage (1). Soil biota, such as worms and moles, help to mix the decaying leaf litter and this helps to maintain soil fertility (1). As well as mixing the soil they also aerate it and prevent the formation of distinct layers in the soil (1). **8**

QUESTION 7: Population

> HINT: Both push and pull factors should be mentioned for full marks.

(a) **Factors could include:**

Turkey is a less developed country than Germany and has a lower standard of living (1). There are few natural resources to be used to increase the prosperity of the country (1). The jobs which were available were mainly agricultural and poorly paid (1). With the increased use of mechanisation even these jobs were disappearing (1). There was little alternative employment available in rural areas (1). There was a lack of education and health care in rural areas (1).

Germany had a labour shortage and needed workers to rebuild its infrastructures especially following the Second World War (1). German people did not want the type of jobs available, leaving opportunities for Turkish workers who were prepared to fill these vacancies (1). Jobs were available in secondary and tertiary industries and these jobs offered the opportunity of earning higher wages (1). These jobs offered Turks the chance of a better standard of living and also allowed them to send money home to their families (1). Also, they would have access to education facilities and health care (1). **8**

> HINT: For full marks both advantages and disadvantages should be mentioned.

(b) **If country of origin is chosen:**

Advantages to Turkey

The Turkish economy benefited from money being sent home to the migrants' families (1). With fewer people in the country pressure was reduced on the limited resources and left more jobs available, thus reducing the unemployment rate (2). Birth rates declined as the migrants were mostly male (1). This meant a decrease in the population, resulting in less pressure on resources, e.g. the food supply (1). When migrants return they bring new skills which can be used to improve conditions in Turkey and its standard of living (1).

Disadvantages to Turkey

Most migrants were young males aged between 18 and 30. This led to a population imbalance (1). In the countryside the villages were left unprotected as only women, children and old people were left (1). This also caused problems as the women were left to try to farm the land as well as look after the children (1). In some cases it was the better educated population who migrated, which hindered the development of Turkey (1). **6**

QUESTION 8: Urban Geography

> HINT: If asked a question on the site and situation of a case study city, you should show that you clearly understand the meaning of these terms and be able to apply them to your chosen city. For example, when discussing a city's growth, as well as referring to factors such as tourism and financial services, you should refer to the significance of its site and situation.

> **TIP**
> For full marks both site and situation must be mentioned. Your answer must refer to a specific city, otherwise you can only receive a maximum of 3 marks.

(a) Glasgow's original site was on the banks of the Molendinar burn at a natural ford in the river (1). The terraces of the river provided an ideal location for early settlement, as it was protected from flooding while having a sheltered location (2). In early times the River Clyde provided food and water (1) and the ford allowed Glasgow to develop as a trade centre as it was a route centre for people travelling from the north to the south of Scotland (2). The River Clyde continued to be influential in the growth

QUESTION 8: (continued)

of Glasgow, whose location on the west coast of Scotland allowed trading with the Americas (1). Its sheltered location and the proximity to raw materials, for example coal in Lanarkshire, led to the growth of the city through the shipbuilding industry (2). Its central location led to it becoming a centre for learning and religion with the establishment of the university and the cathedral (1). The Clyde provided water power and a water source for industry. **6**

> **HINT**: Credit will be given for named examples within the chosen city (up to 3 marks). You would only get a maximum of 4 marks for answers which do not relate to a specific city.

(b) Some areas of the city centre have been pedestrianised, e.g. Buchanan Street and part of Sauchiehall Street (1). This has taken place in order to reduce the number of vehicles in and around the CBD, reducing noise and air pollution (2). It also increases the safety of pedestrians (1). The narrow grid iron streets were under pressure from the increase in the number of vehicles. To reduce this congestion, bus lanes, parking meters and new car parks have been created (2). Areas in the Merchant City have been redeveloped, with old buildings being converted into high quality flats, e.g. Black Friar's Court (1), as well as restaurants, cafes and designer shops (1). These facilities have been developed to attract the young, more affluent population wanting to live and work in the city (1). Other areas have been developed to attract tourists and shoppers into the city, e.g. Buchanan Galleries and the Concert Hall (1). The old bus station at Buchanan Street has been upgraded to try to encourage people to use public transport and to reduce traffic congestion in the city (1). **8**

Exam 2, Paper 2

QUESTION 1: Rural Land Resources

> **HINT**: Questions which provide maps of National Parks should always include reference to the location of parks and detailed explanations of the location by showing the links between the parks and motorways and urban concentrations. When asked about the ways in which the negative effects of tourism can be tackled, make sure you do not write mainly about the negative effects themselves rather than measures used to tackle them.

> **HINT**: If you are asked a question about a case study area and you refer, for example, to the Lake District, for good marks your answer should refer to a named lake, mountain, settlement and perhaps a by-pass road and a park and ride scheme. Try to avoid bland and non-specific details such as using litter bins to solve the litter problem. Try to provide real case study information.

(a) The Lake District is one of the UK's most popular National Parks. It has spectacular examples of glaciated scenery. The upland glaciated areas such as Helvellyn, Striding Edge and Scafell Pike (1) are popular with hill walkers and tourists who climb the peaks to admire the view and take photographs of the surrounding area (2). The many lakes, such as Windermere and Bassenthwaite, provide opportunities for water-related activities (1). Fishing, sailing, wind surfing and jet skiing are popular activities (1). The glaciated valleys such as Langdale are popular with ramblers and people looking for a nice area for a picnic (1). There are many small, picturesque villages, such as Ambleside. This is popular with visitors because the buildings are old and built from local stone (1) and there are tea shops, cafes and gift shops (1). Areas of forestry provide nature and mountain bike trails and opportunities to study wildlife in their natural habitat (1). The area also contains places of historical interest such as Dove Cottage, Grasmere, the home of William Wordsworth, and Hill Top Farm in Sawrey, which is where Beatrix Potter lived (1).

Sheep farming on the steeper slopes and mixed farming on the valley floors provide jobs for farmers and local people (1). Income is generated from the sale of wool, meat and milk (1). Many of the valley slopes are too steep, and the soil too infertile, for arable farming, so livestock are found (1). Forestry is also found on the steeper slopes with infertile soils and this provides jobs in the timber industry and in the paper and furniture industries (1). Tourism is the biggest employer in the Lake District. The park employs wardens and tour guides. The towns and villages have a range of services and facilities for tourists which provide employment for locals on a full and part time basis (2). Local crafts can be sold in souvenir shops (1). Farmers can provide the cafes and restaurants with fresh produce (1). Tourists spend money in the area and some of this can be spent on improving roads and services for locals and visitors as well as helping to stop rural depopulation (2). **10**

Worked Answers to Practice Exam Papers Exam 2, Paper 2: Higher Geography

QUESTION 1: (continued)

> **TIP**
> For full marks the opportunities should be linked to a named landscape feature. Marks can be achieved for naming a specific location (up to 2 marks).

(b) **Limestone pavements**

Joints and bedding planes formed in the limestone as it dried out as pressure was released (1). Limestone was exposed as a result of glaciers moving across the area during the ice age. Abrasion removed the vegetation and soil covering. This left the limestone exposed to the elements (2). This allowed rainwater to penetrate the limestone (1). Rain dissolves CO_2 as it falls, forming carbonic acid (1), which reacts with limestone as it passes through the rock (1). The carbonic acid dissolves the stone, enlarging joints and bedding planes (1). On the surface, chemical weathering widens and deepens the joints to form grykes (1). This leaves raised blocks of limestone called clints (1). Water also gets into the joints, freezes at night and widens the grykes (1). Examples of limestone pavements are found at the top of Malham Cove and at Ingleborough in the Yorkshire Dales (1).

Gorges

Gorges, such as Goredale Scar (1), are thought to have formed when the roof of a cavern became weakened (1). Water permeated the joints and bedding planes, forming underground caverns (1). The roof collapsed when meltwater rushed through the underground system after the last ice age leaving a steep-sided gorge (1).

Swallow/sink holes

Limestone is a sedimentary rock which allows water to seep through it via a series of joints and bedding planes (1). When a stream flows onto limestone it enlarges the joints over which it flows as a result of chemical weathering (1). This is where acid in the rainwater erodes the rock (1). Eventually, when a joint has been enlarged sufficiently, the stream will disappear and flow along underground channels, which have been formed by water dissolving the limestone along joints and bedding planes (2). The stream also erodes the channels by the usual process of river erosion, as rock debris carried by the river results in vertical erosion (1). The point where a stream disappears underground is called a swallow hole (1). A good example is Gaping Gill (1).

Stalactites and stalagmites

These are found in underground caves and caverns. They form in underground caves and caverns where water seeping into the caves via the joints and bedding planes comes into contact with air and loses some of its carbon dioxide (1). This makes the water less acidic (1). The water that seeps down through the limestone is loaded with dissolved lime (1). Where the water drips down from the roof of a cavern or cave a small amount of water will evaporate and leave a tiny deposit of calcite $CaCO_3$ (1). This is repeated every time water drips from the roof, so that in time a stalactite is formed (1). A stalactite is a thin icicle-shaped piece of limestone hanging from the ceiling of a cave (1). In a similar way calcite is deposited on the floor of the cave. As the drips land, the deposits build up to form a stalagmite (1). The splash spreads the calcite so stalagmites are thicker than stalactites. A stalagmite is a stumpy column of limestone sticking up from the floor of a cave (2). Pillars of limestone form when a stalactite meets a stalagmite (1). Examples of stalactites, stalagmites and pillars can be found in the White Scar Caves, near Ingleton (1). **20**

> **TIP**
> Both surface and underground features should be mentioned. For full marks at least three features need to be explained well. Fully labelled diagrams could achieve full marks. Credit will be given for named examples.

(c) (i) **Answers might include:**

Malham Cove is an area in the Yorkshire Dales which is a 'honeypot site' as it has a high number of visitors throughout the year. The area is popular with visitors (especially in the summer months), who come to view the excellent examples of limestone scenery (1), e.g. Malham Scar and the limestone pavement found at the top, as well as visiting Janet's Foss and Goredale Scar (1). The area offers both active and passive opportunities for visitors (1). As the area is part of the Pennine Way it is popular with walkers (1). Walkers and ramblers can walk from Malham Tarn through Watlowes Dry Valley to the top of Malham Cove and from there over to Goredale Scar and Janet's Foss before walking into Malham village (2). The limestone scar at Malham Cove is also popular with rock climbers and abseiling clubs (1). Small villages such as Malham are picturesque (1) and provide services such as toilets and cafes for visitors (1). The less active visitor can stroll around the village and have lunch in the Lister Arms or Buck Inn (1). There are also several places to have picnics (1). There is a National Parks Centre where visitors can get information on the area and other popular areas of the Yorkshire Dales, e.g. Ayrgarth Falls (1).

QUESTION 1: (continued)

There are limestone caves to explore, for example White Scar Caves and Ingleton Cave (1). The area is also popular with pot holers, who explore areas such as Gaping Gill (1). **6**

(ii) **Benefits brought by tourists might include:**

Visitors help to prevent rural depopulation as they have to be provided for (1). They require services and facilities and this helps provide both full-time and part-time jobs for local people (1). These visitors provide jobs in the small villages in the hotels, bed and breakfast places and youth hostels, e.g. Malham Youth Hostel and Beck Hall (1). Farmers can sell local produce to these places and this maintains farms in the areas (1). These farms can also rent out their fields as campsites, e.g. Townhead Farm, and this adds to the farmer's income (1). Local craft industries can sell their products directly to the tourists or via the small gifts shops such as Goredale Gifts in Malham (1). Wardens and tour guides can be employed by the National Parks Authority. Jobs are also provided in local transport as buses operate between Gargrave and Skipton into Malham, especially during the summer months (2). **6**

> **HINT** For full marks both problems and solutions should be mentioned.

(iii) The sheer volume of traffic coming into Malham, especially in the summer months, can cause traffic congestion (1). The access roads are very narrow and were not designed to carry large numbers of cars and large coaches and buses (1). The main access route is very narrow and winding and this can be very busy at the weekends and on bank holidays, as the majority of visitors come by car (1). The car park at the National Parks Centre is quite small and soon fills up. The overspill traffic parks in the village or on the access roads, making them narrower and adding to the congestion (2). This also causes noise and air pollution (1). Park and ride schemes have been introduced to try to reduce the number of cars coming into the area – buses leave from Gargrave and Skipton (1). This has helped to reduce the number of cars on the roads and has led to lower levels of noise and air pollution, but the majority of tourists still want to come by car so they can arrive and leave when they want (2). Farmers rent out their fields as car parks during the busy months and on bank holidays, and this reduces the number of cars parking inappropriately in the village, e.g. over residents' driveways and on the narrow access roads (1). This also makes the farmers money, as they can charge up to £5 for the day (1). Advertising other areas such as Ingleborough, which are a bit quieter, can take pressure off 'honeypot sites' and this has worked to a certain extent but only if there are good facilities and services for the visitors (1). Many still want to visit the more established tourist areas (1).

Footpath erosion is another problem in popular areas. The high numbers of walkers erode the footpaths and the surrounding area as they sometimes take shortcuts, destroying the land and the dry stone walls around the paths (1). The access path into Malham Cove can get very muddy, especially after heavy rain, and people step off the path to avoid the puddles which form. This damages vegetation and plants growing adjacent to the path (2). The paths become wider and the landscape becomes scarred (1). Wildlife habitats can be destroyed (1). Limestone chippings and slabs, which are hard wearing, have been laid on the path to make it more durable and drains have been built at points along the path to stop water from gathering (1). Signs have been erected asking people to stick to the paths (1). At the National Parks Centre there are leaflets on the Country Code (1). Stiles have been built over the dry stone walls to prevent them being damaged as they are expensive to repair (1). Park wardens have been employed and they can monitor the visitors and ask those who stray off the paths to go back onto them (1). All of these things have helped to reduce the problems, as the majority of the visitors are here to see the spectacular scenery and they want to preserve the area. However, there will always be visitors who have little or no regard for the areas they visit. They have just come for a day out. These people have no respect for the people who have to live and work in the area (2). **8**

(50)

QUESTION 2: Rural Land Degradation

(a) The rainfall pattern in the Sahel shows continuous variations (1). Between 1900 and 1950 the rainfall pattern shows a variety of wet and dry years (1). From 1950 to 1970 the rainfall remained above average, with some years being well above average (1). This was followed by extremely dry years between 1970 and 1990 (1). 1984 was a particularly dry year when hardly any rain fell at all (1). From 1990 until the present, rainfall returned to levels slightly below average, but year-to-year variability was high (1).

During the drier periods the soil dries out. This means plants cannot survive (1). With no plants there are no roots to bind the soil together. This allows the soil to be blown away by the wind, leading to land degradation (2). The soil which is blown away is the most fertile layer, the topsoil, so crop yields become poorer (1). As yields become poorer, people are forced to cultivate marginal land (1). Over-cropping and over-cultivation can also lead to degradation (1).

QUESTION 2: (continued)

Land which is bare is also more susceptible to erosion from rain leading to the top soil being washed away (1). Annual rainfall is often now coming in short, intense bursts that destroy crops and seeds leaving the land unprotected (1). However, in times of increased rainfall, crops and animals can be farmed as rainfall allows previously dry land to be cultivated (1). **12**

> **TIP**
> For full marks all three areas must be referred to. You would get up to 6 marks for any one factor. One mark can be awarded for a specific example.

(b) (i) **Deforestation**

The population in the Sahel is constantly increasing. Woodland is the main source of domestic fuel. In the last century almost 90% of the forest was cleared in the Ethiopian Highlands (1). Trees provide a protective cover for the soil. Their leaves and branches intercept any rainfall. When this cover is removed the soil is left exposed to rain and sun (1). The sun bakes the land until it is so hard that any rainfall just washes over it instead of percolating through it (1). The soil is then washed away, leaving large gullies and bare, useless areas (1). Also, when trees are removed, their roots are no longer present to bind the soil together, allowing soil erosion to occur (1). Also, the removal of trees means there is nothing to break the speed of the wind, resulting in large amounts of soil being lost through wind erosion (1).

Over-grazing

In some areas of the Sahel the local tribesmen, for example the Fulani, believe that the number of animals they own reflects their status in the tribe so they keep as many as possible. This leads to the land being stripped of vegetation (2), which leaves it open to soil erosion (1). The rise in the population of the Sahel countries has brought an increased demand for food (1). This has brought about an increase in the number and size of herds grazing in the Sahel. This puts the grazing areas under extreme pressure, especially around wells, bore holes, oases, lakes and rivers, where animals are taken to drink (2). The concentration of herds, for example goats, in these areas results in the vegetation being stripped down to the roots (1). The number of animals trampling the area leads to the ground becoming compacted, which reduces the rate of infiltration of the soil and also increases runoff (1). This allows large areas to be affected by water erosion (1). Farmers are then forced to graze animals on marginal land, leading to degradation of that land and so the desert expands (1).

Farming

As a result of increased demand for food, farmers are forced to increase yields from their land (1). In order to produce more crops the land is no longer left fallow or is given a shorter length of time to recover (1). As a result the land loses its nutrients and becomes infertile (1). With the unreliable rainfall in the Sahel, crops began to fail and the soil became degraded (1). Rising demand causes farmers to cultivate marginal land on the edge of the Sahara. These areas cannot support crops indefinitely so continued cultivation of these lands causes the areas to become infertile, allowing the desert to spread (2). The local people herd animals. The animal dung should be used to fertilise the fields but because the people are so poor they use the dung as a source of fuel. However, by using dung as fuel, the soil is further degraded as it is deprived of essential nutrients, which in turn affects crop yields (1). **14**

> **HINT** For full marks reference should be made to both people and the environment.

(ii) **The impact on the environment**

Over-cropping and monoculture means that nutrients are removed from the soil, leading to the breakdown of the soil structure (1). In Tigray, Ethiopia, it is estimated that soils have lost about 50% of their productivity (1). When trees are removed for firewood, etc, the soil is exposed and easily eroded by the wind, for example the Harmattan (1). Rain, when it comes, is torrential and causes gullies to form, especially when the soil has been compacted by grazing animals (1). These gullies are very difficult to rectify, resulting in more farmland being lost (1). More intensive farming and grazing is reducing the amount of water in the water table (1). In the last 50 years nearly 70 million hectares of the Sahel have been desertified and in Sudan the desert has advanced by 120 km in 17 years (1).

The impact on people

Failure of crops and death of livestock year after year has led to reduced food supply (1). This causes starvation and death, for example in Sudan and Ethiopia in the 1980s (1). Famine occured which leads to increased infant mortality and death rates (1). The degradation of farmland has encouraged the movement of people from the countryside to the city (1). This has resulted in the growth of shanty towns (1). It has also led to the loss of traditional farming methods (1).

QUESTION 2: (continued)

The nomadic way of life is endangered as more and more former nomads move to settle in areas close to oases (1). **16**

> **HINT** For full marks two methods must be explained.

(c) **Contour ploughing**

Contour ploughing is ploughing along the lines of the contours instead of across them (1). The rows formed slow water runoff during rainstorm, preventing soil erosion, and allow the water time to settle into the soil (1). This can reduce the amount of soil lost to overland flow by up to 50% (1). Infiltration rates are greater, resulting in more moist soil, which encourages growing conditions (1).

Shelter belts

In the 'Dust Bowl' of the USA the creation of shelter belts stops the wind blowing across the land, removing the unprotected top soil (1). Rows of trees are planted across the direction of the prevailing wind (1). The trees slow down the wind; the taller the trees the greater the protection (1). The roots of the trees also improve the water retained in the soil (1) and help to bind it together, preventing the soil being blown away (1). **8**

(50)

QUESTION 3: River Basin Management

(a) **Answers might include:**

When rivers are dammed the surface runoff is reduced (1). Dams restrict water flow so there is less water flowing below the dam and into the sea (1). There is increased evaporation from the surface of the massive reservoirs created behind the dams (1). There is less evaporation from the rivers (1) as there is less water in them due to storage in the reservoirs (1). The amount of water infiltrating the ground is altered as a result of storage in reservoirs (1). Infiltration rates are also altered as rivers are diverted for storage (1) and irrigation channels (1). There may be a change in seasonal variations in river levels (1). The level of water tables will also change (1). **10**

> **HINT** Six marks can be given for either physical or human factors. Factors should be relevant to the chosen dam.

(b) **Physical factors**

The dams should have solid foundations to support their great weight (1). The Hoover Dam was built in a narrow valley to reduce the length of the dam and so reduce the costs (1). There was a large, deep valley behind the dam suitable for the formation of a reservoir which became Lake Mead (1). The rock beneath the reservoir and the dam needs to be impermeable to reduce water loss through seepage (1). The surface area of the reservoirs should be as small as possible to reduce evaporation (1). The catchment area needs to produce enough water to fill the reservoirs (1).

Human factors

The dams should be built in areas that are accessible for workers and materials (1). The desert cities of Las Vegas and Phoenix are expanding and close enough to provide a market for the electricity supplied from the dams (1). The amount of people displaced and the amount of farmland lost should be taken into account when locating the dams and reservoirs (1). The cost of payments for relocating people and farmers needs to be considered (1). Flooding historical sites, like the Rainbow Bridge, should be avoided if possible as should sacred burial ground (1). The dams and reservoirs should take into account disrupting present transport routes (1). **10**

(c) **Social benefits**

There is now an improved water supply for drinking as the dams ensure a constant supply (1). Irrigation water allows farmers, for example in California, to grow crops all year round (1). This increases food supply (1). The availability of water can sustain increasing populations (1) especially in the desert cities of Phoenix and Las Vegas (1). The Colorado River provides water for over 40 million people (1). There is a greater availability of electricity (1). The local populations around Lake Mead now have access to recreational activities like water sports, available because of the creation of the Lake Mead reservoir for the Hoover Dam (1). The Hoover Dam is a tourist attraction, bringing not only money into the area (1). The facilities built for the tourists improve the social life of the local populations (1).

Adverse consequences

Many people were forced to leave their homes to allow the flooding of the valleys to create the reservoirs (1). The town of St Thomas was drowned beneath the waters that created Lake Mead (1).

QUESTION 3: (continued)

The people had to be resettled in other areas which were often not as productive as the land they left (1).

Economic benefits

The dams produce cheap HEP which attracts industry into the area, providing jobs and increasing the standard of living in these areas (2). The water and power produced has encouraged the expansion of the cities of Las Vegas and Phoenix (1). The facilities in these cities attract many tourists, bringing money into the economy (1). The availability of irrigation water for farming means agricultural produce increases (1). This extra produce for sale creates more income for the economy (1).

Adverse consequences

The schemes cost a huge amount of money to build and maintain (1). The more irrigation water is used by farmers along the river, the more saline the water becomes (1). At first, when the water eventually reached Mexico it was unusable (1). To solve this problem a huge desalination plant had to be built at Yuma which cost over $300m dollars to build and costs around $20m a year to run (2). Water is very cheap for farmers to buy so much is wasted (1). The cost of delivering water to the farmers is around $350 per acre foot but only costs farmers $3·50 per acre foot so they do not try to conserve it, and this a huge loss to the economy (2). Large amounts of compensation need to be paid out to people and farmers to be relocated as the reservoirs flood their land (1).

Environmental benefits

There is a constant supply of water for domestic use which benefits health (1). The creation of reservoirs encourages wildlife into the area (1). More than 250 species of birds have been counted in the Lake Mead area (1). The reservoirs and dams are seen by some people as improving the scenery and environment (1).

Adverse consequences

The original wildlife in the area has been forced to move as its habitat has been destroyed by the reservoirs, etc (1). There are no longer wild beavers in Tucson (1). The natural landscape has been destroyed by the dams and associated reservoirs (1). The level of Lake Powell is so high that the Rainbow Bridge, said to be one of the geological wonders of the world, is slowly being dissolved by the water (1).

24

> **TIP**
> Reference must be made to all three sections for full marks. Both advantages and adverse consequences must be referred to. Two marks would be taken off for each section missed out. You can receive up to 4 marks for named examples.

(d) **Answers might include:**

The Colorado River runs through seven states of the USA and Mexico. All parties have to agree to the allocation of the Colorado water (1). Different states have different needs for domestic use, agriculture and industry (1). Each state can pass laws regarding water but these can conflict with each other so it needs the federal government to take control (1). Each state must agree to contribute to the cost and maintenance of the dams and reservoirs (1). The legal system in the USA worked in favour of the richest state (California), so it had more power over the water than the other states, which led to conflicts (1). Mexico was unhappy, because being the last area to receive the water, the quality of the water was poor: agreements were needed to sort out who paid for the cleaning of the water, e.g. by the desalination plant at Yuma (2). Also, by the time the water reaches Mexico there may not be enough water left to meet its allocation (1).

6

(50)

QUESTION 4: Urban Change and its Management

> **HINT**
> If the question provides data on 'change', avoid simply rewriting the data rather than analysing it to identify change. If asked to explain why the pace of urbanisation has slowed in developed countries, good answers will include reference to the process of counter-urbanisation. When referring to a specific case study, good answers will show specific knowledge of the area by including named examples of, for example pedestrian areas, under-cover shopping centres, industrial redevelopment sites, etc. When discussing specific areas of a city such as the 'inner city', good answers will show that you clearly understand these terms and that there is no confusion with other areas such as the CBD or urban fringe.

(a) **Answers may include:**

There is increasing urbanisation in both the developed and developing nations of the world. However, the rate of urbanisation is far greater in the developing nations (1). Karachi is the largest urban centre

QUESTION 4: (continued)

of Pakistan with about 12 million people and is growing at a tremendous rate of about 6% which is twice the national growth rate (1). Half of the population growth is attributed to natural growth (1) and the remaining half to a mass influx of people from upcountry and neighbouring countries such as India, Bangladesh, Sri Lanka, Burma and Afghanistan (1). Many people move from the countryside to the city, swelling its population (1). They move to the city in search of new opportunities, employment and better health care (1). As most of the migrants are young they are more likely to produce children of their own, increasing the city's population (1). More health care is available in the city, and better health care reduces infant mortality and increases life expectancy, further increasing the urban population (2). Overseas aid is more available in the cities, thus attracting migrants to the cities (1).

In developed cities such as Glasgow the trend is to move to rural areas, thus reducing the city's population (1). Better transport routes have made commuting from towns such as Strathaven, 26 miles from Glasgow, possible (1). Bigger houses with gardens are very expensive in the city so people with expanding families move to rural areas for more space and affordability (1). Many people now work from home and can commute into the city when necessary (1). Planning restrictions have been placed on the expansion of urban centres in developed countries (1), for example the creation of greenbelt around Edinburgh and London (1).

12

> **TIP**
> Reference should be made to specific cities.

> **HINT**
> All parts of question *(b)* must be answered for full marks. Twelve marks can be gained for part *(b)* (i). It is possible to answer the three parts together.

(b) (i) **Difficulties**

One of the main difficulties which have resulted from the rapid growth of Mumbai is the increase in shanty towns (1). Shanty towns are unplanned and have incomplete water, sewerage and drainage systems (1). Slum dwellers make up 60% of Mumbai's population, approximately 7 million people (1). These towns are built on any space available, even on roads (1). General hospitals in the Greater Mumbai region are overcrowded and under-resourced (1). As a result of Mumbai's size and high growth rate, urban sprawl, traffic congestion, inadequate sanitation, and pollution pose serious threats to the quality of life in the city (2). Automobile exhausts and industrial emissions, for example, contribute to serious air pollution, which is reflected in a high incidence of chronic respiratory problems among the people (2). In fact, most people rely on private doctors, many of whom do not have any qualifications or official training, putting lives at risk (1). There is high unemployment, made worse by large numbers of people arriving each day (1). There is a growth in trading black market goods (1). Drugs, crime and prostitution are common in parts of Mumbai as the urban poor try to survive (1). Wages are poor as there is such a large labour force looking for work (1).

(ii) **Solutions**

To solve the problem of water supply the World Bank has funded development of 176 Primary Care Dispensaries (1). In 1976, the government passed the Urban Land Act, which was supposed to enlarge the area on which middle, and lower, class housing was to be built (1). In 1985, the government tried to rectify the problem of slum dwellings by passing the Slum Upgradation Project (1). It offered secure long-term ownership to slum households on the basis that they would invest in their housing (1). By giving people an interest in their housing and by guaranteeing home-ownership, they hoped to get rid of the slums (1). The government has tried to improve public transport to reduce congestion and pollution (1). The government of the state of Maharashtra is planning to introduce a congestion charge in Mumbai, India's largest city, to relieve the traffic problems that plague the streets (1). Billboards are being used to try to encourage people to leave their cars at home (1). Car pooling is also being suggested (1).

(iii) **Success**

The World Bank Primary Care Dispensaries supply some medical care facilities but these are underused and the necessary water supplies are unreliable (2). There is always too much or too little water, for when monsoon season hits, some slums are submerged knee-deep in water (1). The Urban Land Act has not been successful as the Act has been used not to build affordable housing for the slum dwellers, but to build more upper class housing which has only worsened the slum problem (2). The Slum Upgradation Project has been partially successful but unfortunately the programme targeted only 10–12% of the slum population, those who were capable of upgrading their homes (1). It disregarded those who did not have homes at all (1). By relocating more than 6000 illegal slum dwellings that encroached on land adjacent to the railway tracks, Indian Railways increased its service dependability, speed and safety (1).

20

QUESTION 4: (continued)

(c) (i) One of the main factors responsible for housing change in Glasgow was the condition of the housing stock (1). Much of the city's tenement housing was built in the late 19th century and at the turn of the 20th century to house the large numbers of immigrants coming to the city to work in the heavy industries. They were built by factory owners as cheaply as possible (2). They were built close to the factories and suffered from pollution (1). They were designed to house large numbers of people in as small an area as possible (1). They were poor quality, overcrowded, damp, had no running water outside toilets (1). Many were damaged during the Second World War and the condition of the rest deteriorated (1), for example Maryhill (1). As the city's population increased, new, affordable housing was needed to house the people (1).

(ii) **Solutions**

In the 1960s and 1970s, three main policies were implemented to alleviate Glasgow's housing problems. These were overspill, high-rise building, and comprehensive development, in which whole areas of the city were completely remade (1). Springburn was declared a Comprehensive Development Area in 1973 (1). Few tenements in Springburn survived the wholesale demolition which took place, both for the purpose of new building and also for the clearance of land necessary to build the new Springburn by-pass (1). This policy of demolition is now regarded as short-sighted and wasteful and since the 1980s the policy has changed to one of urban renewal and regeneration (1). Many of Glasgow's old tenements have been refurbished into desirable accommodation, rather than demolished (1). They have been given new roofs and windows and sandblasted on the outside while being given new kitchens and bathrooms inside (1). Not all the original population could be housed in the renovated properties so many new council schemes such as Castlemilk and Easterhouse were built on the outskirts (1). New towns such as East Kilbride and Cumbernauld were also built to take the overspill (1). In the Gorbals, the old tenements were demolished and replaced by high-rise flats (1). In some areas such as the Merchant City new private flats have been built (1).

(iii) **Success**

New council schemes such as Castlemilk were partially successful (1). They did provide people with newer homes with more modern facilities (1). The houses were more spacious and there were gardens for children to play in (1). However, many older residents of the inner city were reluctant to move away from their friends and amenities of the city and families were split up (1). This area was a distance from the city centre so it cost more money and time to travel in and out of the city (1). There were very few amenities in the new council estates (1). High-rise flats were built to replace the original housing in the Gorbals. This was of poor quality and many flats suffered from dampness (1). There was no place for children to play and older people became isolated in their flats if the lifts broke (2). Noise and vandalism also were common (1). These flats were not a success and have since been demolished (1). However, new towns such as East Kilbride have been a success as there were employment opportunities for the residents who were rehoused there and the housing was of a reasonable standard (2). They could also access the city centre via train and bus (1). The refurbished tenements were also a success as the people got to stay in the area they were used to and also got a far bigger, more modern home (2). **18**

TIP
If you do not use a named city in your answer, you will only get a maximum of 14 marks. You would get up to 3 marks for named examples.

(50)

QUESTION 5: Development and Health

HINT
Answers should be explanations. You will get 1 mark for each correctly identified indicator as a ratio.

(a) One social indicator is infant mortality. This is the number of deaths of infants under one year of age per 1000 live births in any given year (1). In developed countries such as the UK, this figure is about 9/1000. This low figure shows that the level of health care within the country is good (1). The majority of babies are born in well-equipped hospitals and given vaccinations in the first year of life to protect them against killer illnesses (2). In poorer, developing countries such as Malawi, infant mortality rates are much higher at 89/1000. This shows that health care, particularly in rural areas, is not good (1) and many children die as a result of problems at birth or from diseases such as cholera and malaria (1). There is also a lack of clean water, and many children suffer from starvation and malnutrition which makes them weak and more prone to illness (2).

Gross Domestic Product (GDP) is an example of an economic indicator. It can show how wealthy a country is as it measures the total value of goods produced in a country in US dollars per capita (1). If GDP is low it suggests very little secondary or tertiary industry (1). In Malawi it is about $320. Most

QUESTION 5: (continued)

of the people work in agriculture, with many farmers being subsistence farmers who do not contribute anything to the economy (2). In the UK the GDP is much higher, at approximately $43,500. This indicates that many people are employed in industry or service industries that bring wealth into the country (1). Countries such as the UK also make money from trade (1).   **6**

(b) Some developing countries, such as Saudi Arabia, have raw materials such as oil which are in demand globally. This allows them to trade with other countries and bring in money which could be spent on improving the country (2). However, the money is not always spent on the people and is controlled by a small percentage of the population who enjoy a high standard of living while the majority of the people remain poor (2). Countries such as Malawi have a high percentage of people employed in subsistence agriculture and this does not bring money into the country (1). Malawi is also a landlocked country, which makes it harder for it to develop good trade links (1). Civil wars and political instability can lead to disruption and other countries will not invest or trade with countries such as Somalia and Zimbabwe (1). Some countries, such as Chad and Mali, suffer from drought. This makes it very difficult to grow food to feed their people, and they get into debt as they have to borrow money to help them instead of investing it in projects such as education and health care (2).

South Korea is a Newly Industrialised Country (NIC) and has developed, as it offers educated, resourceful and cheap labour to foreign companies who invest there (1). This brings money into the country which has been invested in education, health care and developing the infrastructure of the country (1).

Singapore has a deep, sheltered natural harbour and is in a good position for trade. It has been able to develop as a port and has established good trading links with many countries (2). Cheap labour and imported raw materials have allowed shipbuilding and textile industries to develop (1).

Countries such as South Korea and China are known as 'tiger economies' as they have used their entrepreneurial skills to help them develop as commercial centres (1).   **10**

> **TIP**
> Up to 3 marks can be achieved by naming relevant countries linked to correct explanations. A generalised answer will gain only half marks. Marks can be gained for named examples. Referring to different regional differences as well as differences between rural and urban areas is acceptable.

(c) In Brazil the south-east part of the country has a pleasant climate, fertile soils and raw materials. This is a densely populated area and the capital city (Brasilia) is here. The three cities which make up Brazil's 'Golden Triangle' are also found here: they are Rio de Janeiro, São Paulo and Bela Horizonte (2). This area is very prosperous as it has industry and commerce which provide jobs (1) and also help to attract new investment (1). The rich terra rossa soils are ideal for coffee growing and this provides jobs and goods for export, allowing trade to develop (1). Rio de Janeiro has a natural harbour and has therefore developed as a port, allowing goods to be exported which generates wealth (1). The flat land has also made it easier for roads, railways and airports to be built (1). As the area has a large population density the Brazilian government has spent a lot of money improving services such as hospitals and schools in the area (1). Rio de Janeiro also has fabulous sandy beaches such as the Copacabana Beach, and this has helped tourism to develop (1).

The North (Amazonia) is more remote and has a very hot and wet climate, making it very humid. It has a low population density because of the rainforest (1). Soils are poor here as the heavy rainfall leaches the soil, removing nutrients (1). It is less accessible than the south-east because of the dense forest (1). There has been little development in this area because it has been too expensive to develop (1). However, the trees can be exported and large areas are now being cleared for new settlements, industrial development and cattle ranching (1). Jobs are being created here and it is hoped that people from the more crowded south-east will move here. This would encourage government spending and facilities and services would improve (2).

The north-east of the country suffers from migration out of the area because of a lack of rainfall, which makes it hard for crops to grow (1). The area suffers from a lack of energy and mineral resources so the Brazilian government is reluctant to spend large amounts of money in this area (1).

People in the south-east enjoy a better standard of living than the other areas. However, this area attracts many migrants who do find it difficult to get jobs and they end up in favelas on the outskirts of the larger cities such as São Paulo and Bela Horizonte (1). These areas lack basic amenities such as electricity, clean running water and proper sewerage and sanitation systems (1). The people living in these areas are very poor and can suffer from malnutrition and disease. Their lives are very different from the more prosperous city dwellers, who have good educations and well-paid jobs (2).   **10**

> **HINT**
> When answering a question on methods used to control malaria, good answers will refer to realistic measures rather than concentrating on more unusual methods. Answers which refer to the cause of a particular disease must not confuse that cause with those relating to other diseases which have been studied.

Worked Answers to Practice Exam Papers Exam 2, Paper 2: Higher Geography

QUESTION 5: (continued)

> **TIP**
> For full marks, both human and environmental conditions must be mentioned.

(d) (i) Malaria is found in human settlements as the people provide a blood reservoir for the female anopheles mosquito (1) and the houses provide areas of shade where the mosquito can digest her blood meal (1). If the people leave upturned drinking and cooking vessels this provides areas where water can collect, giving the mosquito a place to lay her eggs (1). Irrigation channels, water barrels and paddy fields also provide areas of stagnant water for the mosquito to breed in (1). Malaria needs regular rainfall to provide the areas of stagnant water in which the mosquito lays her eggs (1) and warm temperatures between 15 and 40 degrees Celsius for them to develop and hatch, so is found in areas like the tropical rainforest (1). The heavy rainfall provides puddles and ponds for the mosquito to lay her eggs (1). Areas of vegetation provide the shade necessary for digesting blood (1).

(ii) **Some methods might include:**

Swamps and ponds can be drained to reduce the areas of stagnant water required by the mosquito to lay her eggs in (1). Fish can be added to paddy fields as they will eat the larvae (1). Insecticides such as DDT and malathion can be sprayed in people's homes to kill the mosquitoes as they digest their blood meals (1). In some areas coconuts have been impregnated with Bti bacteria. This ferments inside the coconuts, which can then be halved and thrown into mosquito-infected ponds (2). Drugs such as chloroquine, larium and malarone can be given to people suffering from malaria to ease their suffering (1). Education can help reduce the number of cases of malaria (1). People can cover up at dawn and dusk, use insect repellents such as autan and sleep under mosquito nets sprayed with insecticide (1). Vaccines are being trialled in countries like Colombia (1). Quinghaosu has been extracted from plants in China and has been used to treat sufferers (1).

> **TIP**
> For full marks there must be some evaluation of the measures used to control malaria.

(iii) Draining areas of stagnant water is time consuming and would have to be done regularly. Also the female anopheles mosquito only requires a small amount of still water to lay eggs in so this has not been very successful (1). Adding fish to paddy fields has been quite successful as they are cheap and easy to breed (1). They can also be eaten, providing the locals with a valuable source of protein (1). DDT is harmful to the environment and is now banned in many areas and replaced by malathion (1). This is an oil-based insecticide and more effective but more expensive than DDT, so many poor developing countries cannot afford it (1). People do not want it sprayed in their homes as it stains the walls and does not smell very nice (1). The Bti-infected coconuts are a successful way of eradicating mosquitoes as the larvae eat the bacteria, which destroy their stomach linings (1). This method is cheap and environmentally friendly and a pond can be controlled for about 45 days using only a few coconuts (1). However, this can only be done in areas where there is a plentiful supply of coconuts and some people would say that it is also a waste of a valuable food source (1). The drugs used to treat sufferers have had varying levels of success. Chloroquine is the cheapest of the three but mosquitoes have developed resistance to it so it is no longer successful (1). Larium is very powerful and will help to protect people but it is not popular as it has harmful side effects (1). Malarone is newer and has fewer side effects but is very expensive to produce so it is not used in many poor countries even though it is about 98% effective (1). If people cover their skin at times when the mosquitoes are most active they can stop themselves being bitten, reducing their chances of catching malaria (1). Insect repellents protect the skin as many contain DEET which the mosquitoes do not like. Mosquito nets are cheap and easy to use so they have been more successful than the other two measures (1). Many people see vaccines as being the way forward, as children could be vaccinated at an early age and this could prevent them catching malaria. This could reduce infant mortality rates and would be successful in controlling the disease, provided people got themselves and their children vaccinated (2). Quinghaosu in pill form is being seen by doctors and drug companies as the long-awaited breakthrough, but there is still not enough evidence to suggest that it will be really successful (1). The plant would also have to be grown in large quantities, and in areas outside China, so that pills could be manufactured on a large scale (1).

24

(50)

Exam 3, Paper 1

QUESTION 1: Lithosphere

> **HINT**: If you can provide a suitable diagram(s) which is/are labelled appropriately you will be given credit for this and it could improve your chance of gaining high marks.

(a) **Formation of a stack**

Cliffs are likely to form where the coastline consists of resistant rock (1). A headland is a piece of land which juts into the sea (1). There can be weaknesses in the rock, for example faults/joints and bedding planes, and these are attacked by the sea (1). Chemical weathering can take place because of the salt in the water, which helps to corrode the cliff (1). The sheer force of the waves crashing against the cliff can erode it through hydraulic action (1). This is when lots of sea water crashes against the land, and air and water are trapped and compressed in rock surface cracks (1). When the sea moves away the air expands explosively, weakening the rocks, enlarging the cracks and breaking pieces off (1). The base of the cliff can become undercut through attrition, where stones and rocks are hurled against the rock, wearing it away (1). Through time the weaknesses in the rock become wider (1). A small cave can be formed at the base of the cliff (1). If the water hitting the back of the cave swirls upwards, the roof of the cave may collapse (1). Waves can attack the headland on both sides and erode back to back caves, which will eventually meet and an arch will form (1). During stormy weather or high tides the archway will become weakened (1) and eventually the roof cannot be supported and it collapses, leaving a tall pillar of rock isolated from the headland. This is called a stack (1). An example of a stack is Old Harry in Dorset (1).   **10**

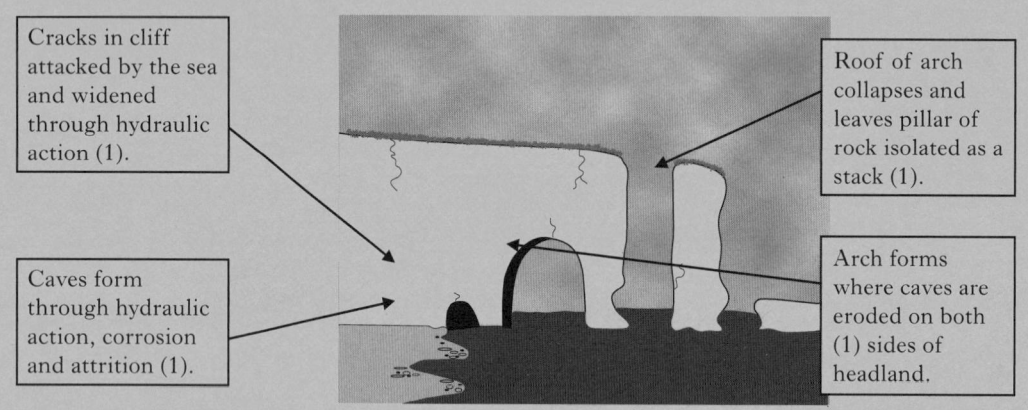

Cracks in cliff attacked by the sea and widened through hydraulic action (1).

Roof of arch collapses and leaves pillar of rock isolated as a stack (1).

Caves form through hydraulic action, corrosion and attrition (1).

Arch forms where caves are eroded on both (1) sides of headland.

(b) Slumping takes place where softer materials such as sandstone and clay are found on top of heavier materials such as shale and limestone (1). When it rains heavily, the water will soak into the more porous rock (1). It soon becomes waterlogged and heavier as the water cannot drain through the impermeable clay (1). Clay is also a soft rock and cannot support the heavier, saturated sandstone above it (1). Rotational movements of large slabs can produce a curved, ruptured surface (1). At the coast the sea can undercut the softer rocks such as boulder clay and slumping will occur (1), e.g. at Lulworth Cove in Dorset, and the land will slip towards the sea (1). Cliffs will collapse and material will pile up at the base and become eroded through time (1).   **8**

QUESTION 2: Biosphere

> **HINT**: For each stage of the transect, you should provide named examples of plants to indicate your thorough knowledge of this topic.

(a) Plants such as sea rocket and sea sandwort will be found at the strandline (1). These plants can survive the strong winds and submersion in sea water as the tide comes and goes (1). They are salt tolerant and sand- and wind-resistant (1). This is why they can survive so close to the sea (1). The conditions here are alkaline because of the presence of shell fragments (1). At the embryo dunes these plants are replaced by species such as sea couch grass and lyme grass (1). These plants have side roots and this helps to bind the soil (1). Sand sedge and sea holly are found in the fore dunes (1). These plants decay, adding some humus to the soil (1). Marram grass can establish itself here as its long roots help to bind the soil together and it can obtain water from the water table (1). This helps to stabilise the dune (1). The yellow dunes are further inland and conditions for plants are better as these areas are further from the sea and are more sheltered (2). At the yellow dune, marram grass is the dominant species as soil fertility has increased and the soil is more acidic (2). As it is xerophytic, it is able to survive the drier conditions (1). As the marram dies, more humus is added to the soil and other species such as ragwort and sea bindweed can be found (2). In the dune slacks, conditions are damper and the slacks are protected by the dunes from the wind, so a wider range of plants is found (2). Some leaching has taken

QUESTION 2: (continued)

place so soils are more acidic and water-loving plants such as cotton grass and rushes are found (2). In areas furthest from the sea, vegetation will be well established and small trees, such as birch and pine, as well as heathers, will be found (2). In areas where there is a high shell content the soils are less acidic and may lead to deciduous forest (1). **12**

(b) Climax vegetation is the final stage in the development of the natural vegetation in any given locale or region (1). Plant communities will change as environmental conditions change (1). Hardy pioneer species will colonise an area first (1). As they die out they add humus to the soil, allowing other plants to grow and survive (1). This is known as succession (1). When this happens, the composition of the plant community is relatively stable and in equilibrium with the existing environmental surroundings (2). This state is normally determined by climate and/or soil (1). When climax vegetation has been reached plants are well established and trees such as pine and birch can be found (2). Biomass is at its maximum (1). **6**

QUESTION 3: Population

> **HINT**: It would be helpful if you could give some examples of the type of questions which are included in the census form.

(a) Accurate population data can be collected by a census. In the UK a census is carried out on a regular basis, every ten years (1). This allows comparisons to be made over time (1). There is a legal responsibility on householders to complete the census form (1). The forms are collected and checked by enumerators (1). The questions are designed to gather information on age, occupation, living conditions and lifestyle (2). In the UK registration of births, deaths and marriages is compulsory (1). A mini census may be carried out in between to update trends (1). Sample surveys are carried out to find out local changes, e.g. General Household Survey (1). **6**

(b) (i) and (ii) **Answer refers to China:**

The size of a country makes collecting census data difficult (1). For example, China stretches over a wide area and takes in huge tracts of desert and mountain ranges (1). The mountains in the south-west form part of the Himalayas, the highest mountain range in the world (1). Poor communication routes mean some places are inaccessible (1). There are also grassland areas which support 'herders' who migrate with their animals (1). It is difficult to collect accurate information for this group of people, wandering across an area half the size of Europe (1). Since it is illegal for many couples to have more than one-child, millions of people with additional children have lied to census takers and hidden their children for fear of punishment (2). People would lose benefits given to them by the government for adhering to the one-child policy so they do not tell the truth (1). The Chinese census includes figures for a neighbouring country (1). Beijing does not control Taiwan but claims the country as part of its territory (1). There are many different languages spoken so many people may not understand the census and so give inaccurate answers (2). **12**

QUESTION 4: Industrial Geography

> **HINT**: Giving named examples of actual industries in the area which you have studied will enhance your answer and gain you additional marks.

(a) Traditional industries, such as the Dalzell Steel Works in Motherwell, were normally located near to the bulky and heavy raw materials needed to produce iron and steel (2). The main source of power was coal, so most traditional industries were located on or near coalfields (1). This reduced the cost of transporting the bulky coal (1). There were many coalfields in and around Lanarkshire, for example at Craigneuk and Auchenheath, to supply the iron and steel works (2). Local supplies of iron ore and limestone were also available for use in the iron and steel works (1). There was a growing market for the steel produced in the nearby shipyards on the River Clyde (1). The final products could be transported abroad via the Clyde, for example to the USA, where there was increasing demand for steel and heavy industrial goods produced in Central Scotland (2). The British Empire also provided a huge market for the coal and steel (1). The Forth and Clyde canal and later the rail network offered good transport links to move the heavy finished products (2). **8**

(b) Modern industrial developments, for example Eurocentral in North Lanarkshire, are footloose industries (2). Access to raw materials is relatively unimportant (1). One of the main factors taken into consideration is the communication network (1). Eurocentral is located next to the A8 leading to the M8 motorway and within easy reach of Glasgow city centre and Glasgow airport (2). There is also easy access to the M74 for transporting goods to England (1). A good road network is also needed to allow easy access for workers (1). A market for the goods produced also needs to be taken into consideration (1). Modern industrial locations increasingly take into account the social needs of its employees (1). Many new industrial areas are designed to be scenic and aesthetically pleasing (1). Many include health clubs and entertainment facilities to ensure the wellbeing of the workforce (1). The industries try to locate near to places where a skilled workforce could be employed, for example from the nearby universities

QUESTION 4: (continued)

of Glasgow and Strathclyde (2). Another important factor is the influence of the government. Many new industrial areas are found where government assistance is available (1). Government grants etc, encourage new industry to locate in areas of high unemployment (1). The EU also has an influence on the location of modern industries as funding is available in designated areas (1). **10**

QUESTION 5: Atmosphere

> **HINT** You must be able to correctly identify the different cells and be able to describe how they were formed.

(a) At the equator, warm air rises and travels in the upper layer of the atmosphere to 30° north and south (1). Here the temperatures are lower, so the air cools and sinks (1). Some of this air returns over the surface to the equator forming the Hadley Cell (1). The rest of the air moves north over the surface and converges at about 60° north and south, with cold air sinking at the poles, which flows outwards (1). The warmer air is forced to rise above the colder air and flows in the upper atmosphere towards the poles, where it sinks and forms the Polar Cell (1). The rest of the air in this layer of the atmosphere travels south and sinks at 30° to form the Ferrel Cell (1). It is in this way that warm air from the equator is distributed to higher latitudes which are cooler, and colder air from the poles moves southwards towards the lower latitudes which are warmer (1). **8**

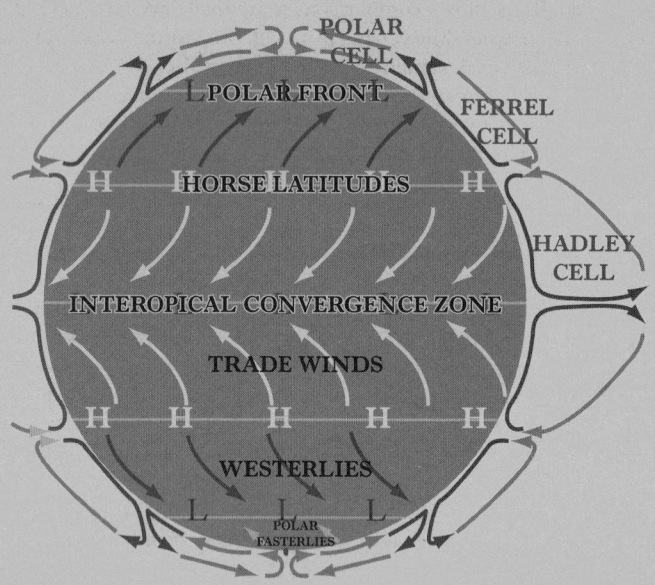

(b) The trade winds push surface water westwards at the equator (1). Here they are obstructed by continental land masses and are deflected northwards and southwards. The currents are pushed eastwards by the westerly winds (2). The Gulf Stream, which originates in the warm waters of the Caribbean is pushed in a north-easterly direction in the North Atlantic by south-westerly winds which blow towards Europe (2). In the northern latitudes this ocean current is known as the North Atlantic Drift (1). This current moves north, away from the equator, and carries warm water into the cooler northern areas (1). On the eastern side of the North Atlantic, the Canaries Current flows back towards the equator (1). Ocean currents move in a clockwise direction in the northern hemisphere and anti-clockwise in the southern hemisphere (1). Due to the earth's rotation, winds in the northern hemisphere are deflected to the right and in the southern hemisphere to the left, helping to create the pattern of ocean currents (1). The Coriolis Force deflects the currents (1). As cold water is denser than warm water the cold water sinks away from the poles and spreads out towards the equator (1) so cold currents such as the Labrador Current are formed (1). **6**

QUESTION 6: Hydrosphere

> **HINT** If a diagram of the hydrological cycle is provided, make use of the information given. If a diagram is not provided and you can produce a labelled sketch, this will improve your chances of higher marks.

(a) The hydrological cycle is driven by the sun and is a continuous cycle (1). This heats water in the oceans and seas and some moisture is evaporated into the atmosphere (1). As the warm, moist air rises, temperatures fall, causing the moist air to condense so clouds are formed (2). Winds (advection) blow the clouds towards the shore where they are forced to rise over high land and rain falls (1). This will fall as snow on higher ground (1). This rainwater flows into streams and rivers and returns to the sea as surface runoff (1). Some of the rain will soak into the soil (infiltration) and return to the system as ground water flow (2). Trees and other vegetation will intercept some of the rainfall and this can be stored in the trees via their root system (2). Some moisture returns to the atmosphere from the trees

QUESTION 6: (continued)

and vegetation through evapotranspiration (1). Some moisture will be stored in glaciers, icecaps and lakes (1). Evaporation will also occur from reservoirs and lakes (1). **6**

(b) The rising limb on the rural hydrograph is not as steep and the peak discharge is lower than the one on the urban hydrograph (1). This is because some of the moisture will infiltrate the ground or be intercepted by the trees and other vegetation (1). In urban areas there are concrete and tar surfaces which allow water to run over the surface into man-made drains (1). This allows water to flow into rivers more quickly, giving a higher peak discharge (1). The lag time on the rural hydrograph is longer (1) as the precipitation takes longer to enter the system as a result of the interception by vegetation (1), such as deciduous woodland (1). Some precipitation will land on leaves and then drip onto the ground (1) and some will infiltrate the soil, so taking longer to return to the river (1). Gutters and drains will return water to rivers quickly via the drainage and sewerage systems in urban areas (1) so the lag time is shorter as there is very little infiltration or interception by vegetation in urban areas (1). The falling limb for the rural hydrograph is gentler than that of the urban hydrograph (1). In rural areas water will slowly seep/return to the river system many hours after the rain has stopped (1). This is because of through-flow via the soil and rocks (1). It will take longer for the river to return to normal base flow (1). In urban areas the river returns to normal base flow much quicker as a result of the manmade surfaces and drainage system (1), so the falling limb is much steeper, showing a quicker return to normal levels (1). **8**

QUESTION 7: Rural Geography

> **HINT**: When answering this type of question always refer to specific locations.

For answers to intensive peasant farming and shifting cultivation see Exam 1 or Exam 2.

(a) **If extensive commercial farming is chosen:**

This type of farming is found in the Prairies area of North America (1). Here the land is flat and the soils are deep and rich in humus (1). The climate has moderate rainfall and summers are warm and dry (1). These conditions are very good for cereal crops, although some irrigation may be required in drier areas in the summer months (1). Monoculture is common, with wheat or maize being the dominant crops grown (1). Crops are grown for sale (1). The flat land means that machinery can be used for ploughing, sowing and harvesting the crops (1). The fields are large, to increase yields and to make it easier for the larger machines such as combine harvesters to turn (2). As this type of farming uses many machines, population density in these areas is low as not many workers are required (1). Farms are not too close to one another (1). In some areas soil erosion from wind is common, especially during the dry summer months, so strip farming is practised (2). This land is ploughed at right angles to the wind and alternating strips of wheat and grass are grown (2). This type of farming also relies on fertilisers and pesticides, which can be costly (1). Crops can be stored in silos, then sent to market in autumn (1). As crops are bulky they are usually sent to market by rail (1). **6**

> **HINT**: You should refer to a named location.

(b) In areas such as East Anglia the fields have been made larger to increase population and improve yields (1). This has led to fences, hedgerows and trees being removed from the landscape (1). Ponds and marshes were also drained to increase the amount of land under cultivation (1). This has destroyed wildlife habitats and the countryside has lost its 'natural' picturesque look (1). This is especially true in areas such as East Anglia (1). Removal of the hedges and trees, which provide shelter from wind for the crops, has also increased soil erosion (1). Their roots also help to bind the soil together (1). This has affected soil fertility (1). Farms have been amalgamated to make them more cost productive (1). This has led to rural depopulation as people have lost their jobs and there are very few job opportunities in the farming areas (1). In East Anglia some set-aside land is now used for camping and caravanning (1). This allows farmers to rest the soil but still have an income from the land (1).

In the Prairies this type of farming relies heavily on machines so less manpower is required (1). Co-operatives now operate within prairies, hiring machinery and labour (1). Some extra farm workers are required at harvest time but only for a few weeks of the year and they are usually 'contracted' in (2). Newer drought- and disease-resistant seeds have been introduced so yields continue to increase, meaning more crops for sale and increasing farmers' profits (2). Some farms have introduced other crops and have diversified, giving them a greater variety of products to sell (1). **8**

QUESTION 8: Urban Geography

> **HINT**: Make sure that you refer to appropriate evidence taken from the OS map provided to support your answer rather than relying on generalised statements.

QUESTION 8: (continued)

> **TIP**
> There would be a maximum of 2 marks for correct grid references.

(a) Area A is adjacent to Sheffield's Central Business District (CBD), which is found in grid squares 3586 and 3587 (1). This is likely to be an older residential area because of its proximity to the CBD, so housing is closely packed and likely to be 19th-century terraces or tenements (2). There is very little open space, and houses do not have front gardens (1). The streets are mainly laid out in a grid-iron pattern (1). There are two main roads, the A57 and the A61, running through the square (1). The B6069 at 341871 and several minor roads are also found here (1). There are five churches and the university at 342872 (2). The housing is close to the services and facilities of the CBD and other services, such as the hospital, at 339870 (2).

Area B is found on the outskirts of Sheffield, approximately 7 km from the CBD (1). Streets are mainly curved or cul-de-sacs, although the A61 does pass through the south-easterly edge of the square at 349800 (2). Housing here is not as densely packed as those in Area A (1). It is likely to be newer, detached or semi-detached, built in the late 20th century (1). These houses will have back and front gardens and they may also have garages (1). There is more open space compared to Area A and a stream flows through the square at 345803. This area also has a golf course (2). There are fewer services but there are schools in adjacent squares, e.g. at 342811 and 355807 (2). There are also two churches in square 3481 and a hotel in 3580 (2).

Area A is less than 1 km from Sheffield's CBD so land is more expensive here than it is on the outskirts of the city as this area is more accessible (2). There is more competition for land and this would explain the lack of open space in square 3487 (2). Housing is built close together to save space and this would also explain the lack of back and front gardens (2). Housing was built close to where people worked (1). This area will be more congested with noise and air pollution because of the main roads which link the outskirts of Sheffield to the CBD (1).

Area B will be quieter and the air will be cleaner as it is further away from the CBD and no main roads pass through the area (1). There is no industry here (1). It will have a more pleasant environment as there is open land with a golf course (1). There is also an area of woodland and more open space nearby in squares 3680 and 3780 (2). Houses will be detached and semi-detached with gardens to the front and rear as land is much cheaper here (1). This is because there is less competition for land (1). The A57 takes people to the CBD and the nearby A6102 links motorists with the A61 and the M1, making it easier for people living here to commute (2). There are fewer services here but the residential area is close to a school and churches in square 3481 (2). Residents prefer the peace and quiet and may feel that it is a better area to bring up their children as streets are quieter and cul de sacs do not have through traffic so it is safer (2). **8**

(b) As the Meadowhall shopping centre is built on the site of a former steel works, there would have been a large area of flat land available for building on (1). The area also had plenty of room for car parks (1). Good communications links were already in place (1). The A6109 and A6107 are close to the shopping centre, and the M1 runs to the north-east with an intersection at 399909 (2). This makes it easier for shops to get products delivered as well as giving easy access to workers and customers (2). There is also a railway station at 390912 and a main bus station at 391912, giving easy access for people without cars (2). The shopping centre is close to residential areas like Wincobank (3891) and Brinsworth (4190) (2). These and other residential areas will provide a workforce and customers (1). Other large urban centres such as Manchester, Barnsley and Rotherham will also provide customers as Meadowhall is accessible via the M62 and M18 motorways (2). The River Don flows past the shopping centre, e.g. at 390910, and the area around it has been landscaped, providing a pleasant, attractive environment for shoppers (2). There is still some derelict land which could be developed to the north-east at 394915, and to the south at 397906 (2). **6**

Worked Answers to Practice Exam Papers Exam 3, Paper 2: Higher Geography

Exam 3, Paper 2

QUESTION 1: Rural Land Resources

> **HINT**
>
> **Land use** If a question asks for discussion of opportunities of the landscape for various land uses, good answers will refer to a variety of land uses such as farming/forestry, recreation/tourism rather than concentrating on one or two land uses. Good answers will also link land uses to aspects of the physical environment.
>
> If discussing conservation strategies, good answers will refer to specific points rather than give a series of general statements.
>
> If a question relates to a specific conflict in land use, good answers will avoid referring to conflicts other than the one asked for in the stem of the question.

> **TIP**
>
> Not every point given in the sample answer below and in the other answers has to be included in your answer. You should have sufficient points to match the number of marks available.

(a) **Answers may include:**

The Lake District National Park is found in the north-west of England. It is easily accessible to a large number of people as it has good access from the M6 motorway (1). Twenty-three million people live within a three-hour drive (1). The park is easily accessible from large conurbations such as Greater Manchester, West Yorkshire and Tyne and Wear (1). It is also accessible via the M74 motorway from Glasgow and the A595 from Carlisle. This allows people to come for the day (1).

It is popular because of the magnificent glaciated scenery (1). Over 15 million people visit the park every year (1). The park offers visitors a variety of activities, both passive and active. For the passive visitor there are pretty little villages such as Caldbeck and Ambleside, which are built from local stone (1). These villages have small cafes and tea rooms for people to enjoy. Gift shops can sell locally produced products (1). These villages also have old churches and in Caldbeck there is an old mill that people can look at, as well as the village duck pond with its wildlife and picnic tables (1). The larger settlements of Keswick and Windermere offer more facilities and services for tourists who not only want to come for the day, but who want to stay longer (1). There are hotels and bed and breakfast places such as the Burnside Hotel at Windermere and the Queen's Hotel in Keswick. This allows people from London and from other countries the chance to stay in the area longer (1). These settlements also have more for the visitor to see and do. In Windermere there are specialist climbing and boating shops as well as souvenir and gift shops (1). There is also the Old Laundry Theatre. In Keswick there is the Pencil Museum and Cars of the Stars Motor Museum. Passive visitors to the area can wander round the settlements stopping off at the many cafes and tea rooms and sample the local Kendal Mint Cake (1).

Along the shores of Lake Windermere and Lake Bassenthwaite are footpaths and people can walk along the shores of the lakes, stopping to admire the view or have a picnic (1). Tarn Hows is one of the most visited spots because of the beautiful scenery. There is a 1·5-mile path around it which is flat and suitable for families with young children and for wheelchair users (1). The area also offers a variety of activities for the more active visitor. The hills and mountains can offer mountaineering, hill walking, abseiling and in some areas paragliding (1). Scafell Pike is England's highest peak at 978 metres and Helvellyn and Skiddaw are also popular areas for hill walkers and climbers (1). People will climb these to admire the wonderful views, photograph them and paint them (1). The lakes can be used for boat trips, jet and water skiing and wind surfing (1). Lake Windermere also offers canoeing, rowing and pleasure boat trips and is the largest lake in the area at 10·5 miles long (1). Mountain biking and orienteering trails can be found in the forest parks, such as Grizedale and Whinlatter (1). As the Lake District offers such a wide variety of activities it also has many facilities like car parks, toilets and information centres for the public, therefore making it more popular than other more remote parks (1). **10**

(b) (i) and (ii)

The majority of visitors who arrive in the Lake District come by car. This can lead to congestion on the main roads and narrow country roads (1). The A595 is a dangerous road and there are frequent accidents on it, which can lead to long tailbacks (1). Tailbacks can increase both noise and air pollution (1). To reduce congestion on some roads, by-passes have been built such as the one around Ambleside, alleviating congestion in the narrow streets in the village (1). Park and ride schemes have been introduced. People can leave their cars and take shuttle buses into the busier spots (1). This reduces the number of vehicles on the roads and has been quite effective but many visitors want to arrive and leave whenever they want so the majority of people still come by car (1). This means that more parking spaces have had to be made in towns and villages and at local beauty spots (1). The car parks at Tarn Hows can fill up quickly and visitors park on verges making access to the area more difficult and also increasing congestion (1). Parking on the verges also destroys vegetation and animal habitats (1). This problem has been

QUESTION 1: (continued)

tackled by putting concrete borders along the verges to make it more difficult for cars to park and has successfully reduced the number of cars parking on verges (1). Local farmers have also rented out fields during the summer months. This is effective and also has created additional revenue for the farmers (1). However, some people will not pay to park their cars and continue to park irresponsibly (1). Some roads have been closed to visitors and can only be used by locals, allowing them to go about their business (1). This pleases the locals and reduces conflicts between them and visitors (1).

The majority of tourists head for the 'honeypot' sites such as Keswick, Helvellyn and Lake Windermere. This can put pressure on these places (1). Over 80% of all visitors to the Lake District will go for a walk. This is a lot of feet treading the paths in popular areas (1). Footpaths on the hills like Scafell Pike and Helvellyn can become eroded because of the sheer volume of walkers on them and the land beside these paths can also become worn away as people take short cuts or step off muddy paths (1). Water running down these paths can also create gullies and erode the path even more (1). This makes paths uneven and difficult to walk on so people step off the paths, damaging the land beside them (1). The National Park Authority tries to repair the popular paths but relies on volunteers helping them to maintain them (1). Footpath erosion has been tackled by trying to make the paths more durable so that they are not eroded as easily. One method is through sub-soiling (1). This creates a solid, hard-wearing surface and requires very little maintenance. It is also cost efficient, costing about £20 per metre (1). It also looks natural so blends well into the surroundings. This has worked and is popular with both locals and visitors as erosion and scarring of the landscape have been reduced (1). Signs have also been erected, asking people to remain on the designated paths (1).

Farmers' fences and dry stone walls can be damaged by people climbing over them (1). This can allow animals to escape and can be expensive for the farmer to repair (1). The dry stone walls at Wasdale Head at the head of Wastwater are frequently damaged by climbers trying to reach Scafell Pike (1). To prevent people climbing over them stiles have been built and this has reduced the amount of damage (1). However, there are still tourists who will not walk to find the stiles, so they still climb over the fences and walls, damaging them and annoying farmers and conservationists (1).

Lake Windermere is popular with water sports enthusiasts as it offers a range of opportunities. There are pleasure cruises which run from Bowness and people can hire rowing boats here. At the Low Wood Water Sports Centre a range of activities is offered (1). People can be taught to sail and water ski here (1). Other activities on the lake include kayaking and jet skiing. Some visitors will also wind surf on the lake (1). However, motor boats and cruisers can pollute the water if they leak fuel (1). People on the boats sometimes also drop litter into the lake, polluting the water (1). Locals and visitors complain about the noise and water pollution from the jet skiers and motorboats, which other water users also complain about (1). They also complain about the speed they travel at (1). This creates larger waves which are eroding the lake shores (1). To prevent conflicts with users, parts of the lake have been zoned off to keep water and jet skiers away from other parts of the lake (1). Speed limits close to the shore have also been introduced (1). The noisy boats and jet skis scare fish and can get caught in the fishermen's lines (1). Lakes such as Haweswater and Thirlmere are reservoirs. Thirlmere supplies water to the north west of England (1). As a result of this, motorised activities are banned so these lakes are more popular with families and walkers who want a bit of peace and quiet (1). There are some water sports like sailing and canoeing as they will not pollute the water in the same way as diesel boats (1).

Litter is a problem in both the popular settlements such as Keswick and Ambleside and in the countryside and forested areas (1). It is easier to deal with in the settlements, as they have bins and these are emptied regularly (1). There are also people employed to pick up the litter (1). People can be fined for dropping litter (1). In the countryside wildlife can be harmed by litter and rivers and lakes can become polluted (1). Decaying litter smells and is unsightly, ruining the very areas people have come to admire (1). **20**

(c) Langdale Valley is an example of a U-shaped valley. This is formed by a glacier moving through a V-shaped river valley (1). During the ice age glaciers occupied river valleys. As a result of gravity the glacier moved downhill, eroding the landscape (1). Large glaciers are very powerful and plucking occurred on the valley sides, making them steeper (1). This is because ice sticks to the rock and pulls fragments away as it moves (1). Material which falls into the glacier deepens the valley floor through abrasion as rocks stuck in the glacier act like sandpaper, making the valley wider and smoother (1). When the ice retreated, a deep, steep, flat-floored U-shaped valley was left (1).

Tributary valleys were occupied by smaller glaciers so were not eroded as deeply as the main valley. After the ice retreated they were left suspended high above the main valley as hanging valleys. Waterfalls are common here (2).

Interlocking spurs were blunted by the powerful glaciers plucking and removing the rock. They were left as steep cliffs at the side of the valley known as truncated spurs (1).

QUESTION 1: (continued)

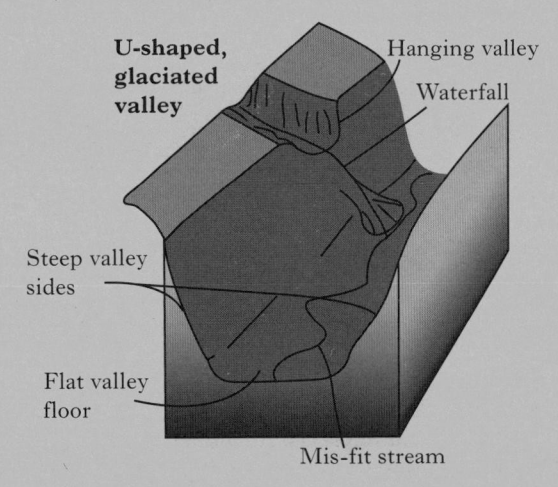

Diagram: U-shaped glaciated valley showing Hanging valley, Waterfall, Steep valley sides, Flat valley floor, and Mis-fit stream.

Corries form when snow collects in hollows on a mountainside, especially in shaded areas (1). The snow turns into ice or neve and begins to move downhill as a result gravity (1). Freeze-thaw weathering (where water gets into cracks in the rock and freezes at night putting pressure on the rock which eventually cracks) (1) and plucking (where ice sticks to the rock and pulls fragments away as it moves) steepen the back wall (1). Material which falls into the glacier causes abrasion on the floor of the hollow as the material acts like sandpaper, smoothing and deepening the hollow to form a deep rock basin (1). As the glacier moves out of the hollow it loses some energy and material is deposited, forming a rock lip (1). When the ice retreats and melts a steep, deep armchair-shaped hollow is left, such as Brown Cove in the Lake District (1). Water can gather in the bottom of the hollow forming a small corrie lake or tarn. Examples of corrie lakes can be seen at Blea Tarn and Red Tarn (2).

When two or more corries form back to back on a hillside, a steep, sharp-edged ridge called an arête can form. Striding Edge is an excellent example of this feature (2). When three or more corries form back to back the landscape is eroded into a sharp point known as a pyramidal peak. Helvellyn is an example of this (2).

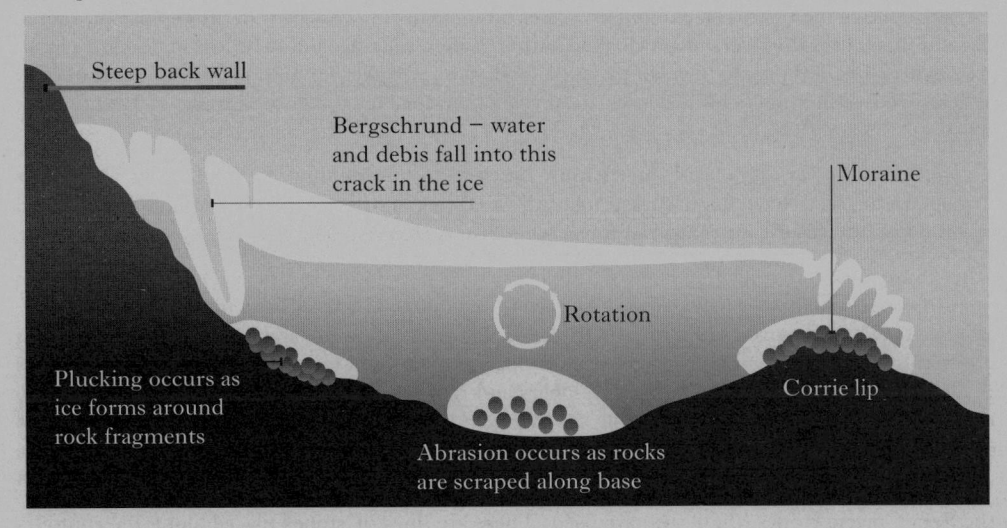

Diagram: Cross-section of a corrie showing Steep back wall, Bergschrund – water and debris fall into this crack in the ice, Rotation, Moraine, Corrie lip, Plucking occurs as ice forms around rock fragments, Abrasion occurs as rocks are scraped along base.

(50)

QUESTION 2: Rural Land Degradation

(a) The three main processes of wind erosion are suspension, surface creep and saltation (1). Suspension is where the smallest particles are picked up, blown off the ground, and then suspended in the air, forming dust clouds (1). The amount of soil being removed is quite small but it contains the most fertile soil and it can be blown for several hundred kilometres (1). Saltation is where the wind causes the medium-sized particles to vibrate, causing them to bounce off the soil surface (1). They are too big to remain suspended in the air, so they fall to the earth and dislodge other particles (1). This process is then repeated. Saltation accounts for between 50% and 80% of soil movement (1). Surface creep is when the largest, heaviest particles creep along the soil surface. Generally they do not move far (1). **6**

QUESTION 2: (continued)

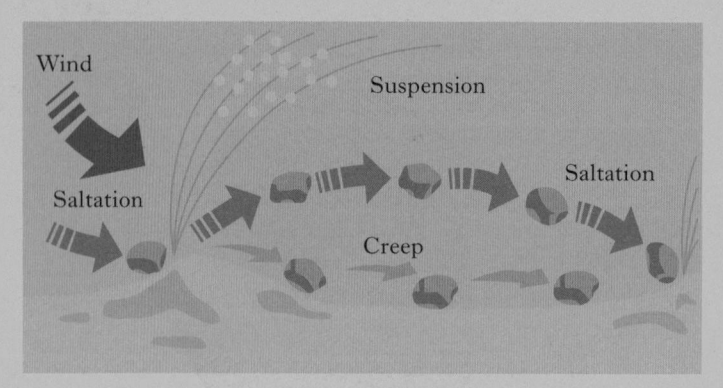

Diagram showing wind erosion processes: Wind, Suspension, Saltation, Creep.

(b) In the Amazon Basin deforestation is the major cause of land degradation (1). Between 2000 and 2007 Brazil lost nearly 150 000 square km of forest (1). Almost a third of recent deforestation is caused by poor subsistence farmers/shifting cultivators (1). The shrubs are removed and the trees felled. These are then burned and crops planted (1). However, the land soon loses its fertility and the shifting cultivators move deeper into the forest for more short-term agricultural land (1). The now infertile land is left for waste or used for small-scale cattle ranching (1). This further degrades the land, as the cattle compact the land and destroy the remaining vegetation (1). The land becomes useless and subject to soil erosion (1). Large-scale cattle ranching involves much larger tracts of land. The land is cleared, then planted with African savanna grasses to feed the cattle (1). The grasses don't grow well as the soil quickly becomes infertile (1). This land is then abandoned and fresh areas of forest destroyed, causing further degradation (1).

Government policies can also lead to increased land degradation. Brazil is a poor country and needs money to improve its economy and reduce its debts (1). It allows large tracts of forest to be destroyed for logging (1). Not only are the trees removed, which leaves areas at risk from soil erosion as there are no tree roots to bind the soil together (1), but logging also causes the destruction of large areas of forest around the logging sites (1).

There are valuable minerals beneath the forest floor and mining process destroys large areas of forest as well as polluting the rivers (1). Mining processes often involve the use of water to remove unwanted debris and this causes the rivers to get clogged with sediment causing land to be lost to flooding (1). In the 1980s over 100 000 people invaded the state of Para to prospect for gold (1). Large areas of land were destroyed as the miners built houses, used vegetation for fuel and cleared tracts of land to grow food (1).

The demand for power and clean water supply has lead to the building of HEP plants (1). These hydro-electric projects have flooded vast areas of Amazon rainforest (1). The Balbina dam flooded some 2400 km (920 square miles) of rainforest when it was completed (1).

Another cause of land degradation is the rapidly increasing population in Brazil (1). Cities such as Rio de Janeiro are extremely overcrowded and people are encouraged by the government to move into the rainforest (1). They are given a plot of land to clear and farm, thus more land is destroyed (1). To gain access to the more remote areas roads were built, for example the Trans Amazon Highway (1). This road allowed large numbers of settlers, developers and ranchers to move into areas along the road to further degrade the land (1). After clearing the forest large amounts of soil were lost through erosion from the heavy rain, for example along the highway it was estimated that up to 40 tons of soil per acre was lost (1). **18**

(c) In the Sahel, magic stones (diguettes) are used. These are lines of stones placed along the contours of the land to trap water from rainfall runoff as well as soil (1). This is particularly useful following the seasonal rainfall in the Sahel (1). During the dry months an impenetrable crust forms on top of the baked soil and without some method of trapping the rainfall the water would run straight off the land (2).

Another method used is animal fences. Animals such as goats, eat anything and graze vegetation down to the roots (over-grazing) (1). This prevents any regrowth so soil without roots to bind it together gets blown away (1). The fences keep the animals out of fragile areas, giving the land time to recover and regrow. Grazing of animals can be controlled, again preventing over-grazing (1). Fencing off areas from animals on a rotational basis means herds can be sustained without long-term damage to the soil (1).

Reducing the size of the herds is another method used, focusing on quality rather than quantity (1). This decreases the grazing pressure on the land. With fewer hoofs trampling the soil it becomes less compacted, allowing water to infiltrate the soil (1).

Education can also be used. Farmers can be made aware of the causes and consequences of land degradation and better methods of farming, for example teaching farmers how to manage the soil using methods such as drip irrigation (2).

QUESTION 2: (continued)

Some of these methods have been successful. Stone lines have little cost (1). Farmers can help each other. In Mali and Burkina Faso this method has been successful and some crop yields have increased by as much as 50% (1). Managed grazing areas are successful if fencing is available and affordable (1). However, agreement needs to be reached by the herders in the area, which is not always possible, for example the settlement of Korr in Northern Kenya (1). In some areas the number of cattle owned is seen as a status symbol so this method is not always successful. Even if education is available, farmers very often cannot afford the techniques being suggested, for example drip irrigation and the use of fertilisers (1).

18

(d) One bad farming practice which contributed to the creation of the Dust Bowl was monoculture (1). Monoculture is when the same crop is grown in the same fields year after year, for example wheat in the Great Plains (1). This results in nutrients being removed from the soil, thus reducing its fertility (1). As a result the structure of the soil is weakened, causing the land to be degraded (1). The natural grasses of the Plains have a dense root structure which holds the soil together. Wheat roots are thinner so the soil is more loosely bound, leaving it vulnerable to soil erosion (1). To prepare the land for planting the fields are deep-ploughed and cleared. This breaks up the structure of the soil and leaves the fine, topsoil particles open to wind erosion (1). The farmers also ignored the natural contours of the land and ploughed across them (1). When it rained the water was channelled into the furrows and the runoff carried soil away with it (1). Cattle are grazed on large areas of the Plains and, as herd sizes increased, the natural grasslands were over-grazed down to their roots, leaving the soil unprotected and open to wind erosion (1). During the 1920s the USA became one of the world's largest exporters of wheat (1). After the First World War there had been a shortage of wheat and the price rose dramatically (1). Farmers were pressurised to produce more wheat, putting more demands on the land, leading to degradation (1). Lack of irrigation during hot, dry periods led to the soil drying out, allowing it to be blown away by the wind (1).

8

(50)

QUESTION 3: River Basin Management

> **HINT**: You should try to provide named examples of rivers and river basins for your chosen area to illustrate that you have a good knowledge of the area you have studied.

(a) Most of the river basins in Africa lie south of the Sahara Desert (1). There is a lack of drainage basins in North Africa (1). The only major river basin in North Africa is the River Nile, which flows north through Egypt and drains into the Mediterranean Sea (1). The White Nile drains from Lake Victoria while the Blue Nile originates in the Ethiopian mountains, fed by the higher precipitation levels (1). The Blue Nile joins the White Nile, becoming the Nile (1). In Central Africa, the Niger, Benue and Volta Rivers drain southward into the Gulf of Guinea, while the Senegal River drains west into the Atlantic Ocean (1). The Congo River starts in the mountains of the East African Rift (1). These rivers are fed by high rainfall caused by the equatorial climate in this region (1). In South Africa, the Zambezi and the Limpopo flow in an easterly direction and drain into the Indian Ocean (1).

10

> **HINT**: If data are provided in a resource, try to make good use of it to illustrate the points you are trying to make in your answer.

(b) Water resources in Egypt are limited. There is a low annual rainfall total, with many areas receiving less than 250 mm per year (1). The waters of the Nile are fully exploited and groundwater sources are being used to maintain a water supply (1). The rainfall is unreliable and seasonal in nature (1). At times there is drought and at other times flooding (1). There is a need to store water in times of surplus to enable a constant water supply throughout the whole year (1). The yearly inundation caused by snowmelt in the mountains and heavy seasonal rainfall needs to be controlled to avoid loss of life and destruction of farmland (1). The surplus water can be stored and transferred to appropriate areas to provide irrigation water for crops to grow in the dry season (1). The population of Egypt is growing rapidly, increasing the demand for fresh water and the need for an increased food supply for the growing population (1). Expanding cities and the developing industries need more and more water (1). Better water supply also reduces disease and improves living standards (1). A constant supply of water improves the possibility of navigation, thus increasing trade (1).

10

(c) **Social benefits**

The flooding of the river is in the main controlled so there is less loss of life, property and farmland (1). Droughts are much less likely so people have a constant and reliable source of drinking water (1). A constant supply of fresh water leads to less disease and better health (1). There is more food available as water is available all year round to grow crops (1). The reservoirs provide opportunities for recreation in a desert area (1). The dams produce electricity, increasing its availability to more people (1).

Adverse consequences

Dams and reservoirs take up a lot of space. 90 000 Nubians were forced to move from their traditional lands as large areas of land were flooded behind the dams to create reservoirs (1).

QUESTION 3: (continued)

Irrigation is being used on a regular basis and this is leading to an increase in water-related diseases such as bilharzia (1). This disease is spread by the bilharzia snail which thrives in the irrigation channels (1).

Economic benefits

A constant supply of water allows farmers to grow crops all year round (1) and the use of irrigation has doubled the cultivable area in Egypt, thus increasing output (1). This results in a surplus which can be sold and improves Egypt's balance of payments (1). The production of HEP attracts industry into the area, creating job opportunities, e.g. the steel industry (1). Also the water can be used in industrial processes (1). The money produced by HEP from the Aswan Dam has paid for its construction 20 times over (1).

Adverse consequences

These water schemes are very expensive, e.g. the Aswan Dam cost over $1 billion US to build (1). Egypt is a poor country and relies on foreign aid, which can lead to further debt (1). The more irrigation water is used, the more saline the soil becomes (1), especially further down the river at Cairo and Alexandria (1). This has led to salt infiltration in the Nile Delta which has affected the sardine industry (1). Since the river is controlled, the land is no longer fertilised by the flooding river deposits (1), thus leading to the need to buy expensive fertiliser to keep up the soil fertility (1).

Environmental benefits

There are increased fresh water supplies which improve health and sanitation (1). In a desert area the dams and reservoirs can be seen as improving the scenery (1). The new reservoirs attract new wildlife into the area (1).

Adverse consequences

Ancient historical sites such as the Abu Simbel temple are being destroyed by the rising waters (1). More industry leads to more water pollution (1). The land no longer receives its fertility from the annual inundation (1). The reservoirs collect the silt, reducing the storage area (1). There are detrimental effects on wildlife at the water margins, e.g. wading birds, reptiles and aquatic mammals (1). **24**

(d) The waters of the Nile flow through several countries. Therefore arguments can occur as to who has control over the water (1). The countries lower down, such as Egypt, are dependent on the goodwill of their neighbours upstream, e.g. Ethiopia, as 86% of the Nile's water comes from there (1). If the river/lake becomes polluted in one country then this pollution can be transferred to another country, e.g. Lake Nasser lies in northern Sudan and southern Egypt (2). It is difficult to get cooperation among all the countries using Nile water, as legislation is not always accepted in all affected countries (1), e.g. Egypt and Sudan did not include Ethiopia in the 1959 Nile Agreement (1). Egypt also blocked funding which would have allowed irrigation and HEP projects to go ahead in Ethiopia (1). There can be less water available in some areas than others and future demands are difficult to predict (1). **6**

(50)

QUESTION 4: Urban Change and its Management

> **HINT**: If you are asked to refer to a city you have studied, include references to specific places, districts and industrial areas to show that you know the city well.

(a) The original site of Glasgow was on the banks of the Molendinar burn at a natural ford in the river. This allowed access to both sides of the river (1). The terraces of the river provided an ideal location for early settlers as they protected the early settlement from flooding while giving a good sheltered location for dwellings (1). The River Clyde also provided food and water (1) and the ford allowed it to develop as a trade centre for people travelling from other parts of Scotland (1).

When trade with the American colonies opened up Glasgow was in an ideal situation, being on the west coast of Scotland, with the Clyde giving easy access to the Atlantic Ocean (1). The Clyde was also deep enough to allow large ships to travel up the river (1) bringing raw materials from the Americas, encouraging the growth of the textile and tobacco industries (1). There were raw materials found close by, for example iron ore and coal in Lanarkshire (1), and this encouraged the growth of heavy industries like shipbuilding along the River Clyde, allowing the city to further grow (1). **8**

(b) (i) The main reason why the Glasgow Harbour Development was needed was to regenerate the area along the River Clyde from the SEEC to Yoker (1). Up until the 1970s many of the industries which Glasgow depended on for its prosperity were located along the river, especially shipbuilding and its associated industries (1). Although there are still some shipyards on the Clyde, for example BAE Systems in Govan (1), most are now closed and large areas on the banks of the river are now redundant (1). The land around the river became underused, vacant and neglected (1), for example Meadowside Granary and Yorkhill Quay (1). The derelict land encouraged crime and vandalism as well as discouraging any investment in the area (1). The closure of the shipyards

QUESTION 4: (continued)

and associated industries led to high levels of unemployment in the area (1) and since most of these people had no other skills they found it impossible to find alternative employment (1). Much of the housing in the area was poor and in need of updating (1). Young people were forced to leave the area to look for jobs (1), resulting in the area becoming more run down (1). New types of jobs were needed to bring people back to live and work on the river (1).

(ii) The old docks, and sites of old granaries, for example Meadowside Granary, wharves and shipyards in the area, have been demolished (1), and are being redeveloped into up-market residential apartments, office complexes and leisure facilities (1). This has improved the visual appearance of the area and also made way for a better use of the land (1). Part of the scheme was to build new housing which was affordable and appealing (1). New housing has been built on the old granary site, with up to 2005 housing units by 2010 (1). This new housing has improved the quality and variety of housing in the area and has attracted many new people into the area (1). New businesses have moved into the area, for example car dealerships (1), reducing the unemployment rate and encouraging people to move into the area (1).

The road system has been improved to reduce congestion (1) and two new footbridges have been built. One links Glasgow Harbour with Partick across the expressway and the other is a bridge across the Kelvin (2). These are extremely useful as there are now better transport links between the communities of Glasgow Harbour, Partick and the West End (1), making the waterfront, public space and facilities at Glasgow Harbour more easily accessible (1). The improvements also bring the train, bus and subway services at Partick into easy walking distance for the people who live in, work at and visit Glasgow Harbour (1).

A new transport museum is being built on the derelict land at Pointhouse Quay (1). 42% of the area is designated for new parks, river walkways and cycle routes (1). The Clyde Walkway has been completed along both sides of the River Clyde and gives the citizens of Glasgow and visitors the opportunity to experience new water-based activities in a quality environment (1). **16**

> **HINT**
>
> When answering a question on differences in growth rates between ELDCs and EMDCs note the following:
>
> Weak answers often concentrate on population change rather than the differences in growth rates, which is what the question is really about.
>
> Where questions provide a resource with information about ELDC countries but ask you to refer to a country you have studied, you will fail to score marks if you simply base most of your answer on the resource provided.

(c) Jakarta's population continues to grow faster than New York as Jakarta is a developing city (1). Its natural increase is far higher and each day many migrants arrive in the city, constantly increasing the population (1). Also, since most migrants are young adults, they are more likely to have children, thus increasing the population even more (1). The better facilities available in Jakarta means babies have a better chance of survival than in the countryside, thus increasing the city's population (1). Many people move from the countryside to the city as they think the city offers them more opportunities than the countryside (1). Lack of jobs, water, education and health care pushes people from the countryside and into the city (1).

On the other hand, in New York people are moving out of the city in search of a slower pace of life (1). The towns and villages around New York have a greater natural increase than New York as people from New York move to these areas to gain better accommodation and start families (1). There is limited land available in the city allowing for growth so people move out for a better lifestyle (1). The location of jobs is also a major factor causing outward migration. As jobs decentralise into the suburbs, many workers move to the suburbs (1). Also accommodation can be too expensive in the city so people choose to move out (1). **12**

(d) **Problems**

As Indonesia continues to urbanise at a rapid rate, more and more slums will emerge (1). Over 200 000 to 300 000 people come to Jakarta every year to look for opportunities, exacerbating the already poor conditions (1). In these slums the housing is poor, made from any materials that can be found (1). These areas are overcrowded, have inadequate water supplies, poor sanitation, disease, no electricity and few amenities (1). In Kelurahan Penjaringan, one of Jakarta's largest slums, clean drinking water is a luxury for the families who live here (1). Diseases such as malaria, dengue fever, cholera and acute respiratory infection are on the rise because of contaminated water (1). In this slum, the humid climate of Jakarta adds a layer of stench as there is a lack of developed sanitation plans (1). Many families rely on communal areas for washing and bathing, because they do not have access to their own water supply (1). The main water supply is from a well, and the well water is often polluted and not drinkable (1). Safe water is expensive and the urban poor of Jakarta can spend up to 25% of their entire income just on usable water (1). The shanty towns are often found on unstable hillsides, along railway tracks or beside rubbish dumps (1). In Jakarta, the Cilincing area shanty town of the Indonesian capital lies next to a crematorium and facing the sea (1). Living so close to the water, the area is regularly flooded but with a poorly constructed drainage system and no barriers from the shoreline (1), floods bring more

QUESTION 4: (continued)

than just knee-deep dirty water (1). Skin problems, fever and respiratory infections are common (1). There is little employment and the jobs which do exist are poorly paid (1). There is a black market economy and a problem with crime and drugs (1). The sites are illegal and could be bulldozed at any time by the city authorities (1).

Advantages

There are some advantages to living in shanty towns. The conditions may be better than living in the countryside (1). There are more job opportunities in the city so money can be earned and sent back to family in the countryside (1). The housing is low cost, in many cases free, as the shanties are built from scrap material (1). There are no regulations or planning permission needed (1). A community spirit may develop among the residents (1).

14

(50)

QUESTION 5: Development and Health

(a) The Physical Quality of Life Index (PQLI) uses more than one development indicator and therefore gives a more balanced view of the level of development in a country (1). Indicators such as average life expectancy, adult literacy rates and infant mortality rates are used to calculate the PQLI (1). It is measured on a scale of 0 to 100. If a country's PQLI is below 77 the country is said to be poorly developed (1). Average life expectancy is how long a person is expected to live (1). It can reflect the standard of living in a country. In the United Kingdom (UK) the average life expectancy is 78 years and in Sierra Leone it is less than 40 years (1). The UK is a wealthy country and can afford to look after its people (1). Levels of health care and education are good (1). A healthy, educated workforce helps a country to develop (1). The UK has well-paid jobs in the secondary and tertiary sectors so this brings money into the economy (1). In Sierra Leone the majority of the people are poor (1). They are involved in subsistence farming and find it difficult to feed themselves and their families (1). There is also a lack of clean drinking water, so people become ill and cannot work (1). This makes it hard for the country to develop (1).

Literacy levels measure the ability to read and write. In developed countries such as the UK literacy levels are 99% whereas in Sierra Leone they are only 35% (1). Where literacy rates are high it means that the country has money to spend on building schools (1). It is also able to train teachers and buy materials like books and equipment (1). In the UK it is compulsory for all children to attend school between the ages of four and a half to sixteen (1), whereas in the poorer countries a smaller percentage of children attend school beyond primary level (1) as they are needed to work on the land or look after elderly family members (1).

Infant mortality rate is the number of children who die before their first birthday per thousand of the population (1). It can reflect the level of health care available in a country. In the United Kingdom infant mortality rates are low (about 5/1000) compared to Sierra Leone, where figures are much higher at 155/1000 (1). This reflects the level of health care in a country. Rich countries can afford to build and resource hospitals and train doctors and nurses (1). The level of health care throughout these countries is good, whereas in the poorer countries, the level of health care can vary (1). In the large towns and cities the level of health care is better than it is in the rural areas (1). These countries have limited money to spend on health care so tend to spend it in the urban areas (1). The people in the countryside receive more basic care and they are more prone to illness as there is little access to clean water and the people are more prone to disease (1).

Taking all of these measures together gives a more accurate insight into levels of development and makes it easier to compare countries, as single indicators can be too generalised and do not reveal variations within a country (1).

8

(b) Some developing countries have resources which are in demand globally (1). This allows them to trade with other countries and bring in money which can be spent on improving the standard of living for their people (1). Malaysia has rubber, tin and palm oil (1). Countries such as United Arab Emirates and Saudi Arabia have oil but in some of these countries profits are controlled by a small percentage of the population (1) and very little is spent on improving life for the majority of the population (1). Other countries such as Burkina Faso lack resources and this hinders development as they have very little to sell or trade with (1).

Countries like Mali have a high percentage of people employed in subsistence agriculture, and this does not bring money into the country (1). It also suffers from drought, making it difficult to grow food to feed its people (1). They become ill and cannot work (1). The government has to borrow money to help their people survive (1). They do not have money to spend on education and health care which could help them develop (1), as they are too busy paying off their loans (1).

Taiwan and South Korea are Newly Industrialised Countries (NICs) and earn large amounts of money from industries such as car manufacture, toys and electrical equipment (1). They have educated, skilled workers (1) and labour costs are low (1). The sale of these goods abroad brings money into the countries, and this is invested in education, health care, and developing the infrastructure (2). Singapore has a deep, sheltered natural harbour and is in a good position for trade (1). It has been able

QUESTION 5: (continued)

to develop as a port and has established good trading links with many countries (1). Cheap labour and imported raw materials have allowed shipbuilding and textile industries to develop (1).

Civil wars and political instability in countries such as Somalia and Rwanda can lead to disruption, and other countries care reluctant to invest or trade with them (1). Bangladesh suffers from frequent flooding and cyclones. Instead of trying to develop its resources and infrastructure, money has to be spent repairing the damage caused by these natural disasters (1). This makes development difficult and other countries are reluctant to invest there (1).

Jamaica and Thailand have attracted tourists who spend money in the countries, boosting the economy (1). Tourism also provides jobs for the locals in the hospitality sector and they can also sell local wares to them (1). Money generated from tourism can be invested in the country, helping to improve the standard of living for the people, and the country will develop more (1). **12**

(c) Primary Health Care (PHC) strategies have been introduced in developing countries in an effort to improve the health of the population. In Malawi, 80% of the population live in rural areas where access to clean water, health care and basic sanitation is very limited (1). In 2008, Village Reach, a rural health care programme, was set up in the village community of Kwitanda (1). Village Reach's programme aims to reduce the number of cases of malaria and children suffering from diarrhoea (1). They have distributed long-lasting insecticide-treated mosquito nets to prevent people being bitten by female anopheles mosquitos while they are asleep (1). They also offer advice through trained health workers on general health and hygiene which will prevent people catching malaria or suffering from diarrhoea (1). They have also tried to improve the supply of clean water in villages by building wells and water pumps (1). Improved sewerage and sanitation systems have been installed (1). Local health workers are called Health Surveillance Assistants (HSA) and they work with the local people in treating simple ailments (1).

Lifeline Malawi are trying to improve maternity care in Kasese and this will help to reduce the infant mortality rate of 71/1000 (1). They also have a clinic in Ngodzi which offers eyesight and hearing tests, minor surgery and vaccinations to the villagers (1). The Rosetree Maternity Clinic gives women advice on family planning and offers birth control advice (1). It also provides antenatal and postnatal care to these women (1). This will help to reduce the population, but also help babies to survive, reducing the infant mortality rate (1).

AIDS is a major problem in Malawi. It is said to be the major cause of death for people between the ages of 20 and 29 (1) and approximately 86 000 adults and children die from every year (1). Antiretroviral therapy (ART) is poor in rural areas (1). Médecins Sans Frontières (MSF) have been working in the Chiradzulu District in Southern Malawi since 1999 (1). In this district, 25% of the adult population is HIV positive (1). They opened a clinic where sufferers can come for treatment. The clinic also offers advice on safe sex, issues contraceptives and offers counselling to locals (1). In 2001 a hospital was opened and this helped to treat more people. Community health centres were also opened, which meant that more people could be treated effectively (1).

If Malawi can improve the health of its population, life expectancy will improve (1). They will also have a healthier workforce who can help to develop the country (1). More children will survive infancy, and, if they can go to school, become skilled workers (1). Money generated from the sale of goods can be spent on further development programmes improving the standard of living for the people (1). **10**

(d) (i) Trying to reduce the number of female anopheles mosquitoes can help (1). Areas of stagnant water can be drained as this is where the mosquitos lay their eggs (1). Insecticides such as DDT and malathion can be sprayed on areas of stagnant water and in people's homes (1). This kills the mosquitoes (1) but they are becoming resistant to DDT, locals do not like the smell and it is also expensive (1). Bti bacteria can be grown in coconuts. These are then halved and thrown into ponds where the larvae eat the bacteria (1). It destroys their stomach linings and ponds are protected for 45 days (1). Coconuts grow well in tropical climates so there is a plentiful supply and there is no damage to the environment (1). Releasing dam water every five to seven days drowns larvae as the force of the water gets rid of areas of stagnant water (1). Putting egg whites on the surfaces of stagnant water suffocates the larvae by clogging up their breathing tubes (1). Eucalyptus trees can be planted as they help to soak up excess water through their roots, reducing puddles and pools of water (1). Fish can be added to paddy fields as the fish eat the larvae, are easy to breed and add protein to locals' diet (1).

Primary Health Care programmes can help reduce the number of cases of malaria through education programmes (1). They can ask the people to stay indoors at dawn and at dusk, when the mosquitoes are most active (1), teach them to turn buckets and pots upside down, so that water is not caught, and also teach them to cover human waste, as both will reduce areas for breeding (1). They can issue antimalarial drugs like chloroquine and larium which help people suffering from malaria as long as they take them as instructed (1). They can give people mosquito nets sprayed with insecticide as this stops them being bitten when they are asleep (1). They can also get people to use insect repellent containing Deet as this will protect them against bites if they reapply it at regular intervals (1). **10**

QUESTION 5: (continued)

> **HINT**: Wherever possible in your answer try to provide specific examples of named countries and specific health care projects which you have studied.

(ii) In Malawi development is hindered as treating the disease is costly (1). The government can spend almost 40% of its budget on fighting malaria (1). If the disease could be controlled, more money could be spent on other things. More schools and hospitals could be built (1). Money would be available to improve housing and sanitation for the people (1). The Village Reach programme could have more money to spend on providing clean drinking water (1), reducing the occurrence of other diseases such as cholera (1). Malawi loses productivity as people are often too ill and weak to work. If people were not ill with malaria and cholera they would be fitter and could work (1). This would increase productivity and more food could be grown (1). People would be better fed, more children would survive and infant mortality rates would fall (1). Families could become smaller as there would be less need to have lots of children in the hope that some would survive (1). More children could go to school, obtain a good education and get more skilled jobs (1). This would help the country to develop. Surpluses could be sold, generating trade and providing more to improve the infrastructure (1). Tourists would come to Malawi if the threat of catching malaria was reduced (1). This would create thousands of jobs and generate much-needed revenue (1), helping the country to improve the standard of living of its people (1). They could also develop their secondary and tertiary industries (1). **10**

(50)